3520364380

D1180408

TRAINING YOUR FOAL

TRAINING YOUR FOAL

Schooling and Training Young Horses

by Renate Ettl

CADMOS EQUESTRIAN

For my parents, who taught me to regard animals as fellow creatures and to respect their ways.

Copyright of orginal edition
© 2000 Cadmos Verlag
This edition © 2002 Cadmos Equestrian
2. printrun 2005
Translated by Konstanze Allsop
Layout: Ravenstein Brain Pool
Front cover photo: Christiane Slawik
Inside photos: Renate Ettl
Print: Westermann, Zwickau
All rights are reserved.
Copying or storage in electronic media is permitted
only with prior written permission from the publisher.
Printed in Germany.

ISBN 3-86127-904-5

CONTENTS

THOUGHTS ON BREEDING A FOAL

There can be no greater pleasure for any horse lover than to raise your own foal. Watching the young horse grow, building up an intimate relationship with it, and training it yourself is a matter of much enjoyment. The advantages of raising and schooling a young horse are obvious. The animal does not have an uncertain past, has not passed through many other hands and has thus been spared any bad experiences. Most horse lovers know only too well that correcting a horse is always dangerous and far more time – consuming than training a young, unspoilt horse. A horse's memories of bad experiences can never really be completely erased. Once a horse has been spoilt, it will in the future almost always react with mistrust and panic.

In addition, the raising of a foal strengthens the relationship between man and animal considerably. Most horse owners have a more intimate relationship with the foals they have raised themselves than with those horses which they bought as fully trained mounts. It is true, of course, that such a special relationship can also develop in cases where horse and owner have been through hard times together – be it illness, injury, behavioural problems or other problems to do with care or training. However, the trainer is hardly likely to deliberately bring about such occurrences in order to achieve a closer relationship. It is simpler, more pleasurable and certainly recommended to raise a young horse if your aim is to have a special relationship with it.

But building a satisfactory relationship of mutual trust with a young horse is, however, dependent on requirements which not every horse lover can fulfil. The young horse's living conditions must be such that it can develop its character naturally and is able to act on its impulses. This point alone is one where many horse lovers fail. Shabby compromises do not, in the long term, lead to the much desired enjoyment, but rather condemn to failure the attempt to raise and school a foal in a horse-friendly way.

Anyone who toys with the idea of raising their own foal, or of buying a weanling or yearling, must realise that optimum breeding conditions provide the basis for a happy and healthy horse. In particular, this means breeding within a group of horses where all playmates are of the same age and where there is plenty of light, air and space to run around. Of course the medical care of the foal must also be ensured. Regular worming, vaccinations and hoof care are high on the list of breeding priorities. If all these requirements are fulfilled, then the adventure of raising and schooling a foal can begin.

No horse owner need fear that the period between birth and backing is ever boring. There is a multitude of practical activities with which to occupy the foal. All of these exercises contribute towards the animal's adult life. The better the preparation, the easier it will be for the horse to find its way into its role as a riding horse. Backing will be accomplished with the greatest of ease – with the correct preparation, saddling the horse for the first time will come naturally and the first hack will not be a traumatic event but rather a natural progression following on from the handling of the previous two to three years.

It goes without saying that the pleasure of raising one's own foal will be even greater if not only the rearing conditions are perfect but if the correct choice of dam and sire are taken into account in advance, ensuring the best prerequisites for a healthy and capable foal. The choice of sire and dam should aim to bring together similar types, as this will increase the chance of passing on desirable qualities and minimise the risk of nasty surprises and disappointments. Parents which do not match well often produce foals which are in disharmony and which ultimately nobody wants. The health of sire and dam should also be ensured, since many illnesses, or at the very least the predisposition to them, are hereditary. The probability that a foal will suffer from allergies, eczema, or navicular disease for example is greater if the transmitter (or worse still both parents) is already prone to those types of complaint.

It is never possible to know, despite an optimum mating, which character, weaknesses and conformation faults the foal will inherit nor which gender, size and colour it will be. Therefore, the purchase of a yearling or a two-year-old can, under certain circumstances, be a more practical solution, compared to breeding from your own mare or buying an as yet unborn foal. It is important to realise that it is almost impossible to breed the ideal horse. Breeding your own dream horse is a matter of luck, despite the optimum choice of parents.

Whether you decide to breed your own foal or purchase a yearling or two-year-old, early education always forms the foundation for any riding discipline the horse will be used for in adult life. This book aims to accompany the owner of a young horse from the newly born foal's first hours through to the time when the saddle is placed on its back for the first time and then to the backing of the horse at approximately three years old. At the same time the owners of two- and three-year-olds

may still make use of the lessons of the weanling. The exercises can even be repeated with older horses which have been ridden, and may also be used as lessons for horses which were unaccustomed to them in the past. In the horse's education it is never too late for an exercise, but it can be too early. There are so many types of exercises specifically for young horses that it is not necessary to subject them to lessons aimed at more mature animals. To do so would risk long-term damage, and the handler would not be demonstrating how much his horse can do, but rather how little he understands his horse.

The most difficult aspect of horse training and education is applying the correct amount. The horse owner must be able to make demands of the young horse which are appropriate for its age, but not to overface it.

> Proceeding too hastily with the education of the horse can cause lasting damage through psychological or physical overfacing and demonstrates not how much the young animal has learned to do, but how little expertise the horse owner has.

Quite a few breeders and horse lovers are of the opinion that the foal should grow up more or less wild. In their view, it will have to obey people's instructions soon enough and work for them as a riding or driving horse. This idea is justified to a certain extent, particularly as it can never be too late to educate the horse. But

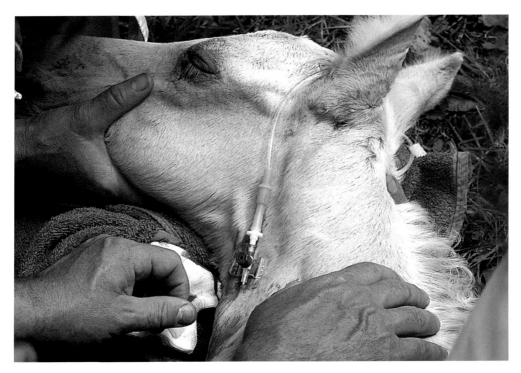

A certain amount of schooling and training is necessary even at an early stage of a suckling's life, in order to be able to ensure that possible necessary medical procedures can be carried out without any problems.

there are some situations which clearly contradict this opinion. What is to happen if the foal injures itself in the paddock and needs medical attention? Or what if the blacksmith has to undertake corrective farriery and the foal will not permit anyone to touch it, just because it is unused to human intervention?

These incidents illustrate that a certain amount of schooling and training is practical even for a young suckling. Other lessons (such as "lungeing") may, on the other hand, be too early for a two-year-old. Only by adhering to a sensible order of events and a correct approach to the various stages of learning, can there be any guarantee of happiness and relationship with the animal. This forms the foundation for a long and healthy life for the horse. The reward for all the troubles of accepting the horse's nature and complying with the requirements associated with this is contented horses and happy owners.

HANDLING THE NEWLY BORN FOAL

A FOAL IS BORN

The birth of a foal is a wonderful experience which no breeder would want to miss. All the same, mares do not like being watched during the birth. They are able to delay the birth for a considerable time if they feel disturbed.

Spending the night in the stable in order not to miss the birth could lead to the mare postponing the birth; therefore it may be recommended to continue the usual daily routine, so that the mare feels secure. However, a certain monitoring of the event must be ensured, in order to be able to help if there are any complications at the birth. When a birth is imminent it is possible to check on the mare every one or two hours, but it would be better to have video-surveillance, although this is an expensive option which is usually only worth the investment for larger breeding establishments. Each horse owner has different pre-requisites and you need to decide from case to case how to monitor the mare with as little disturbance as possible. It is a good idea to have the mare foal in a field, insofar as the surroundings and weather permit, because this enables the owner to keep watch over the mare from a distance without being noticed. During the night the possibilities for observation are limited, so it is better to bring the mare into the stable in the evening.

It is natural to foal within the herd, but this should only be contemplated if the relationships in the herd are harmonious and there has been no friction caused by rank order or the like. In addition, sufficient space must be available so that the foaling mare is able to withdraw a little when the birth starts.

In principle, the area where the birth will take place should be kept as clean as possible. However, this does not have to mean that disinfectant is sprayed by the can. The field or stable will never be germ-free, which is why Mother Nature has ensured that the foal receives antibodies from the colostral milk. Nevertheless, thorough cleaning is necessary to prevent infections affecting the mare and foal. There is no harm in scrubbing the stable thoroughly with soapy water and removing the droppings three times a day. A thick bed

of straw should be prepared in the foaling box after cleaning.

SIGNS OF THE IMMINENT BIRTH

Horses take a relatively long time to foal normally. The pregnancy lasts between 330 and 350 days. The extra 20 days can seem a very long time if the foal is expected with anticipation. But it is still quite normal for horses to carry the foal beyond the expected time by up to 10 days, so there is no reason to be concerned. However, should this period of time be exceeded the vet should be contacted.

Horse owners who know their mare well will notice a "withdrawn" look in the days immediately before the birth. The mare becomes quieter and feels the need to distance herself. Signs of the imminent birth are also drops of resin on the mare's udder bulging with milk, as well as a "dropping" of the tummy and sharp caving in of the flanks. These signs do not always appear, but they do occur in many cases, so it is worth paying attention to them.

Immediately before the birth the mare becomes restless, may walk about nervously, and starts sweating. It is recommended not to feed the mare excessively once you observe signs of the imminent birth, because full intestines can complicate the birth. However, mares often restrict their food intake themselves shortly before birth, which in itself can be a sign. Many stables have a period of quiet after the

If you know your horse, you will notice a "withdrawn" expression on her face shortly before the birth. This mare foaled within ten hours of the photograph being taken.

evening feeds and mares often give birth during this period. However, the majority of foals are born during the night, as this is the time in which the mares have the necessary rest for foaling.

THE BIRTH

The vast majority of foal births occur without complications and the mare giving birth does not require human assistance. Therefore there is no reason to panic or to become nervous when the time of the birth draws closer. Indeed, any display of excitement and nervousness can cause so much unrest that it simply disturbs the mare and may lead to a delay of the birth. If it is possible to oversee the birth almost totally without being observed, this should be the approach, in order to further decrease the chance of complications during birth. In the event that problems do arise, for example, if the foal is lying in the wrong position, rapid help must be available in order not to endanger the lives of mother and foal. Naturally, the telephone number of the vet should be at hand for this eventuality.

After the birth of the foal the needs of the mare must not be forgotten. Now there are two horses to look after accordingly.

The supply of antibodies by way of the colostral milk is discontinued after a few days and the foal will then only receive "normal" foal milk.

Everyone wants to witness the actual birth of a foal. Of course there is no objection to this, but the possible distractions connected to such an action must not lead to the normal sequence of the birth being endangered. Consideration for the mare must take priority over personal curiosity.

The actual birth begins with the mare becoming restless, breaking out in sweat and often lying down and standing up again. Finally, the pregnant mare lies down on the straw and begins to press, in order to force out the foetus. First, the foetal membrane bursts, releasing a large quantity of amniotic fluid. The rupturing of the foetal membrane can also take place while the mare is still standing. Subsequently, both front hooves appear as well as the foal's muzzle, which rests on its front legs. If only one leg appears, or if the two rear legs appear first, the foal is lying incorrectly and the vet needs to assist.

Once the front legs and the head have come out, the mare usually takes a little break to recover her strength before the next stage of labour of pushing the foal's chest through the birth canal. As soon as the foal's trunk is on the straw, the young animal begins to breathe. When the foal has emerged completely, it normally remains attached to the mare by the umbilical cord for a few more minutes. This is a good thing too, as it continues to supply the foal with important nutrients and blood during this phase. Even if the foetal membrane has not yet ruptured, the foal will not suffocate as long as the umbilical cord is intact. Nor-

mally the foetal membrane ruptures by itself, or the mare instinctively bites it open. If neither happens, the foetal membrane needs to be torn open by hand in order to expose the foal's nostrils. Once the mother stands up after a short resting period, the umbilical cord will tear off and the foal needs to be able to breath on its own. At this point, the foetal membrane must have been removed.

The whole birth process normally takes no longer than 30 minutes. After a period of recovery the mare will lick her newly born foal dry. This allows the mare to remove any mucus from the foal's nostrils and eyes. In addition, the licking process stimulates blood circulation. At this point it is possible to assist the mare with a straw wisp which is used to dry off the foal. This first human contact intensifies the foal's trust and facilitates its later education. In addition, you can use this opportunity to disinfect the umbilical stump.

Despite the great desire to care for the foal, the mare should not be forgotten. In her case, particular attention should be paid to see that the afterbirth is discharged completely. This normally happens within 45 minutes. If this process takes longer than two hours, a case of "afterbirth retention" is present. In this case the vet must be called in urgently. Check that the afterbirth is complete. The size, weight and colour of the afterbirth will tell the vet something about the birth process. At the same time the veterinary surgeon will also gain an idea of possible irregularities. Therefore it is advisable to show the vet the afterbirth for his expert opinion. After a further ten to twenty minutes the foal will make its first attempts to stand up. It may fall flat on its face a few times until it manages the first unsteady steps. Trying to stand up is a strenuous task, so a few breaks lying on the straw will be needed. After an hour at the most, the foal should have found the mare's udder and have its first drink. With the first mouthfuls the foal receives milk which is enriched with important antibodies to guarantee the foal's passive immunity. The foal enters the world without any protection. It is very important for the foal to drink the colostral milk as soon as possible in order to receive the protective antibodies. It is therefore quite practical to offer assistance, particularly to weak foals, to help them find their mother's source of milk as quickly as possible. After two to three days the supply of antibodies from the colostral milk ceases and the foal then simply receives "normal" foal milk as nutrition.

MEDICAL CARE OF THE FOAL

Unfortunately, the antibodies which the foal receives with the colostral milk are only effective for the first three weeks. Afterwards, the foal is at a greater risk of developing infections. The foal starts to produce its own antibodies at the age of about three months. Only at this stage, when it has developed its own active immunity, can the foal be inoculated. It is rec-

ommended to inoculate against tetanus, influenza, rhinopneu-monitis and, if required, rabies. The important thing is that the foal receives a correct basic immunisation in order to maintain sufficient protection by vaccination. If the foal is inoculated too early, the inoculation could be ineffective if the youngster is as yet unable to produce its own antibodies. The correct balance of time must be adhered to. This applies to the start of the inoculations as well as to the basic and repeat immunisations. It is urgently recommended that the foal is inoculated against foal paralysis within the first 24 hours of its life. Although this disease is relatively rare, the foal can suffer from intestinal mucosa or a bacterial infection of the umbilical cord, which within the first three days of life can lead to the so-called early or late paralysis, the latter of which develops after a few weeks.

Correct medical care of the foal by means of inoculations and regular worming is essential.

In order to guarantee the health of the foal, it should be wormed for the first time at the age of about two weeks. Worming is then repeated after a few weeks with a suitable medicine. In general, foals need to be wormed more often than grown horses.

The extent of worm infestation depends primarily on the way the horses are kept. Worm infestation usually intensifies in proportion to the number of stock. Hygiene in the stable is another important factor which determines whether the level of worm infestation is high or low. Therefore, regular (daily) mucking out of the fields and paddocks should be a matter of course. In any case, the foal is infected with endoparasites with its first mouthful of milk. No horse is completely free of worms. Regular worming can only reduce the number of worms and keep them at a low level. Unfortunately these parasites cannot be exterminated entirely. Excessive worm infestation can trigger a variety of illnesses, weakens the immune system, and can lead to irreparable damage to the organs. This damage can even result in the death of the horse. Regular sampling of the dung for worm infestation, carried out by the vet, gives an indication of the intensity and type of worm infestation. This ensures the correct choice of a suitable worming preparation for an effective worming and thereby a guarantee of the foal's well-being.

IMPRINTING

The belief that a foal can only be taught very little could not be further from the truth. Every living creature learns an enormous amount in the first hours and days of its life. The main things it learns are survival-related matters. This process of fast learning is called imprinting. We can make use of the process of imprinting in order to teach the foal things which it would learn only with difficulty later on. It must be stated in advance at this point, however, that opinions on imprint training vary greatly. Some horse lovers are of the opinion that foals should grow up more or less naturally and in the "wild" and that humans should only intervene in the youngster's life when necessary (i.e. for medical care). Others view the use of the foal as a primary concern (after all the animal was bred to become a riding horse) and take every opportunity to make the handling of the horse as easy for them as possible. Both opinions have their merits, and as is so often the case, steering a middle course is the right thing to do.

A certain amount of imprinting is certainly practical and appropriate (and is in any case unavoidable when the foal is raised under human supervision). It makes handling the horse easier for you and helps minimise the fear of the foal towards the environment it has been born into. Nevertheless, an exaggerated imprint training can lead to the horse being degraded, to having more or less no will-power of its own: hence the term "push-button horse". It is questionable whether the real horse lover would find any satisfaction in this. Therefore, the question of whether the foal can lead a natural life at all, based on a meticulously planned imprint training, should remain a point of discussion with a large question mark behind it.

WHAT IS IMPRINTING AND IMPRINT TRAINING?

The behavioural scientist Konrad Lorenz was the first to define the term "imprint". In his book, "Ethologie der Graugans" ("Ethology of the Greylag Goose") he explains: "The term imprint indicates a process of acquisition, which ensures that behaviour is bound to a certain object." Imprinting is a fixation period which starts in the first minutes of life and remains embedded forever. Obvious signs of imprinting are the irrevocability, or at least extreme difficulty in deleting the impressions gained. The opportunity of imprinting is limited to very few phases of development, and to merely present a stimulating situation is insufficient to create imprinting. Konrad Lorenz also discovered a further remarkable aspect of imprinting. Imprinting not only

A certain amount of imprinting with humans is certainly practical in order to simplify the handling of the young horse.

relates to the individual of a species, which is the origin of the stimulation for fixation, but to all creatures of this type. This means that an imprint-trained foal bonds more intensely with all humans and not only with the person who carried out the imprint training. With regard to the relationship between the horse and its trainer, this is an important piece of knowledge.

Imprinting is the simplest learning process for humans as well as for animals. This learning process is pre-programmed through instinct and not linked to any type of mental effort. Therefore, the phrase "learning without intelligence" is also used. Animal psychologists call any form of inborn behaviour "instinct" and the ability to learn certain types of reactions "intelligence". It is possible to imprint certain stimuli in all animals within the first few minutes after birth. At a later stage, the animals would have difficulty in learning the reaction to such stimuli if the imprinting phase had not been used. In order to imprint an animal, each species requires a different set of stimuli-

> Imprinting is the simplest process of learning, so it is customary to speak of "learning without intelligence".

depending on the individual behavioural systems.

The aim of imprint training in horses is to make it easier to handle the animal, primarily by containing the instinct of flight and desensitising the foal to various stimuli which would normally frighten it and set it fleeing. In addition, one wishes to strengthen the bond with humans in order to build up respect and trust. At the same time a lasting subordination of the foal is achieved with regard to humans.

Being in contact with the foal shortly after its birth means that you will automatically be imprinted in the young animal's memory. As a consequence, the horse will not fear humans later in life. Since imprinting takes place with humans, animals or objects, which are present in the direct (perceptible) vicinity of the newly born foal, the mare would naturally withdraw in the wild in order to give birth to the foal in seclusion. In this way, she is initially the only living creature near the foal, so that imprinting takes place with the mother alone. Mares in-foal, who are under human care, also seek the peace and seclusion they need to give birth. The mare wants to be alone during the foaling process – her best chance to ensure that the foal imprints on her in the first few minutes of its life. It is generally accepted that the foal will imprint on a large object within the first few minutes, which it will then follow instinctively, as soon as it can walk. Usually, and under normal circumstances, this large "object" is the mother. Konrad Lorenz carried out a test with geese: goslings also imprint on "large objects", which they recognise after hatching from the egg.

Again, this is usually the mother which the goslings will eventually follow. If the eggs, however, are incubated artificially and there is no mother present after hatching, they choose the "next-best" individual in the vicinity to follow. If this happens to be a human, the

The term instinct means any form of inborn behaviour, such as, for example, the horse's flight reaction.

chicks follow him wherever he goes. In the future, the chicks will always be fixated on humans and will never choose to follow any other goose. The goslings do not in fact recognise that they themselves are geese. They regard the human being as their mother, because they imprinted on him/her when they were born.

The same phenomenon can be observed with horses. A horse owner from my neighbourhood fulfilled his dream of owning his own foal after having his only mare covered. Unfortunately, the mare died during birth and the foal was laboriously brought up with the bottle. The horse lover cared selflessly for the little filly and soon the animal grew to become a stately horse. The horse was very devoted, loving and friendly and showed promise of becoming a good mount. Then one day the mare was put into a field with other horses. The supposed benefit of being able to mix with other creatures of the same species turned out to be mistake. The horse did not seek any contact with its own species and the other horses did not accept the mare into their herd. The owner couldn't understand what had happened. His mare was so agreeable and friendly – why was it driven off by the others? The answer is simple: The horse had imprinted on the person and all its later training was also performed solely by humans. It had no sufficient command of the horse language and neither did it know how to get on with its fellow beings. She did not see herself as a horse so she did not seek any contact with other horses but was fixated on humans. The consequence was an incorrect development of the horse. This led to emotional and psychological problems. The horse was "atypical of its species" and became difficult to handle and remained unpredictable for the rest of its life, despite its earlier friendliness.

Experiments with dogs and cats have also shown that animals do not know how to approach each other, if they have been imprinted on other species. The English behavioural scientist, Professor M. W. Fox, for example, smuggled puppies into a cat's litter during the imprinting phase. The mother cat did not have a problem accepting and raising the puppies. Later, however, the dogs brought up by the cat were only able to play with cats – not with dogs.

Imprinting in the first few hours and days of life is an extremely important event, which will impact on the entire future life of the animal. Therefore horse owners and breeders have an enormous responsibility regarding the newly born foal of not committing any mistakes during imprinting, which might have serious consequences. They must be fully aware of the effect certain stimuli can have on the newly born foal. Imprinting of the foal on humans definitely has certain advantages regarding the handling and training of horses. However, the individuality of the horse, as well as natural instincts and behavioural patterns must be respected. Purposeful manipulation through imprint training endangers the horse's respect for the individual as well as for the characteristics of the whole species.

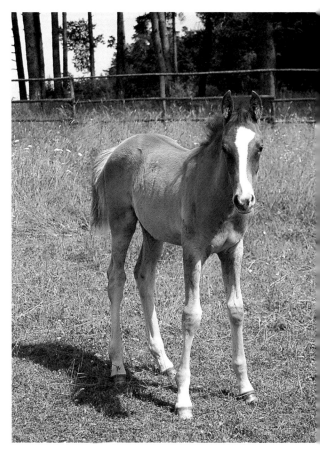

Raising a single foal without any contact with other horses leads to a faulty development of the horse as it is imprinted solely on the human. At a later stage, the foal will be unable to interact with other horses.

Imprinting of a foal on humans has undeniable advantages. However, its natural instincts and patterns of behaviour must be respected

THE TECHNIQUES OF IMPRINT TRAINING

There are four main goals to achieve with purposeful imprint training:

· A better relationship and bonding with humans.

· The sustained dominance of humans over the horse (or the subjugation of the horse).

· Accustoming the horse to certain stimuli (desensitisation).

· Sensitisation towards other chosen stimuli.

It is doubtful whether people who manipulate an animal through purposeful and targeted imprint training have in fact any respect with regard to the species in question.

The vet Dr Robert Miller has systematised imprint training and issued actual training plans for newly born foals. He was the person who made imprint training popular in Europe. Let us take a closer look at his methods: Dr Miller believes that the newly born foal bonds with everything which it registers within the first hour of birth. This assumption coincides with Konrad Lorenz and his discoveries about his greylag geese, and also with the findings of many other behavioural scientists. Normally, the foal first registers the mare, but possibly also any human being who may be present to assist with the birth or who is just curious to get to know the foal. This bonding will take place quite independently from the feeding. Although the foal drinks its milk from the mare, it may also imprint on the person. Imprinting removes the fear which the foal would normally experience. In the wild, it is the mother that the foal trusts and will seek protection from if it is afraid of anything. If imprinting does take place with a human, then the foal will automatically trust that person. It will seek protection in its closeness and will naturally experience no fear of humans. The practical matter is that the foal can bond not only with its own mother but also with the human. However, I am convinced that the primary bonding with another being can only occur with particular intensity to one single individual – and this "intensive bonding" should always be with one of its own species, that is, the mare. This alone guarantees the normal mental development of the foal as a horse.

The second purpose which can be achieved with imprint training is the subjugation of the foal with regard to humans. Since horses are gregarious animals, it is quite natural for them to be dominated by other horses. Otherwise, the pattern and rank order of their herd could not function.

Dominant animals try to settle into the rank order as near to the top as possible. To do this they must fight and always be on their guard. But they have the say within the herd, they get to eat and drink first, and determine the route the herd will travel. The animals which are lower in the order avoid the dominant horses and assume their rightful places below them. But the horse with a lower rank is by no means unhappy in its role. Just like a subordinated person, it feels quite secure within its herd, as the more dominant horses will lead it to the best grazing and will protect it. In this way they benefit from each other. As long as every member of the herd knows its place in the rank order, the community will function as a whole. It is, therefore, quite legitimate to dominate horses, because it is a natural feature for the animal to be dominated. Humans must be higher in the rank order than the horse; otherwise, there would be a great risk of accidents and injuries when the animal is being handled. Dominance does not, however, mean that the horse is physically or mentally broken in, which used to be the order of things and some crude trainers still adhere to this principle today. Breaking in has to do with force, and whether this is physical or emotional is neither here nor there, training to overstep the limits of domination and to subjugate the foal, primarily on an emotional level. The tiny

The herd structure cannot function unless a rank order has been established.

The owner fits a headcollar on the foal at the same time as the dam is approaching. Due to the fact that the foal cannot move away it signals its subordination through distinct chewing.

horse has no opportunity to defend itself so shortly after its birth: it is weak and helpless and, therefore, at the mercy of humans, without any chance of resistance. The trainer should always take this fact into consideration when thinking about imprint training.

Horses themselves prove that dominance has nothing to do with physical strength. It is not an infrequent occurrence that an old weak mare leads the herd and is quite capable of putting a young rascal in its place. The lead mare achieves this through her mental

Foals which have learned to trust humans of their own free will, rather than having been manipulated to this end by force during the imprinting phase, make better companions for those humans.

strength, which gives her the ability to dominate other horses. Humans need to confront the horse – be it dominant or subordinate – with the same mental strength. Only then can the horse be dominated without physical effort or brute force. This would not require imprint training. However, there is a method which assists the subordination of horses.

Inferior animals display their most vulnerable point to their opponent, in order to show that they cannot resist and are helpless. In a way, they beg for mercy with this gesture ("Please don't hurt me"). A dog, for example, will roll onto its back and show its vulnerable stomach. In the case of foals (sometimes also with older horses) a chewing action can be observed. Some experts interpret this imitation of eating as the following expression: "Please don't do anything to me, I am a herbivore and am not interested in attacking you". An alternative interpretation of this behaviour, which is a more tempered definition, is: "I do not want to fight with you, I just want to eat". Whatever the correct answer, this type of behaviour is to be observed primarily in foals, a sign that especially the foal shows a great readiness to be dominated – this being quite logical for the youngest and weakest member within the herd.

When do animals show their subordination? Primarily this happens when they are deprived of their strongest weapon and thereby become defenceless and weak. The horse's strongest weapon is its ability to escape in flight. It is an imperative weapon of survival for horses in the wild. If the horse is unable to flee, however, it is at the mercy of its enemy (or the situation it finds itself in). If a person prevents the horse from running away, it is fairly helpless with regard to said person. For the animal, this means dependence and obedience as well as respect for the more dominant creature. These characteristics are of great advantage when dealing with horses.

Many training methods depend on this behaviour. Some horse trainers, for example, use the method of hobbling (tying together of the front legs) solely to make the horse submissive, obedient and subservient – not, primarily, to prevent it from running away, for which purpose tying up the horse in a headcollar is the preferred option. Hobbling is a means to an end. It practically renders the horse's legs useless. In the wild this would mean certain death. In the hands of a human this spells absolute dependence.

Horses which can no longer escape try to defend themselves by kicking or biting if they feel threatened. If this is prevented (for example, by tying the legs or hobbling), the horse is completely helpless. In the case of the foal there is a simpler method to make it defenceless: by simply holding it down on the ground and not letting it stand up. In this position it is unable to flee and the fact the humans are dominant will be imprinted indelibly in its memory. This is a basically logical, but questionable method, as the foal no longer has a choice to make a decision. It is forced into this situation. I interpret this method as a form of breaking the horse's will. In my experience, horses which choose not to run away and stay voluntarily, turning to humans with trust, are the better horses. For this reason I prefer to use the foal's inborn trust and natural inquisitiveness, gained through the early bonding with the youngster. If I then, in addition, take on the role of the lead-mare I automatically have lasting dominance over the horse - without resorting to forceful methods.

> Horses which choose to trust humans of their own free will, make better companions than horses which have been manipulated and "broken in".

In order to be able to use the horse as a riding horse, it makes sense to desensitise it to certain stimuli, and on the other hand sensitise it towards other stimuli. The horse, for example, should be desensitised towards cars, tractors and rustling plastic tarpaulins so that it has no fear of them and, therefore, will not cause problems for the rider (and itself) through possible panic reactions. On the other hand the horse should be sensitised towards the aids in order to enable the rider to ride in a sensitive manner. Desensitising training is carried out on horses of every age whenever they are sacked out (see also p.108 ff.). However, Dr Robert Miller prefers to get even newly born

foals used to the sound of plastic bags, loud motors and shearing equipment, so that the animals have no fear of these things later on. He also desensitises newly born foals to every type of touch.

For the purpose of desensitisation, the specific stimulus has to be repeated as often as necessary, until the horse shows no defence reaction, or it becomes clear that the horse has become indifferent to the touch. To do this the stimulus must be applied between 30 and 100 times. If this stimulation is stopped too soon, a sensitisation will take place to a certain degree, but no habit will have formed. The result would be to achieve the opposite of what one intended. In practice, a form of body massage is performed on the foal when using the technique of Dr Miller. This also includes touching all its orifices. Working in the foal's mouth should prepare it for wearing the bit. The finger is placed into the nostrils 30 – 100 times in order to make the possibly necessary introduction of a nose-gullet-probe easier. The fingers are pushed into the outer ear and the anus (this is intended to make taking the temperature easier). Repeated knocking on all four hooves is intended to help the foal get accustomed to shoeing. Throughout the whole procedure the foal is held down on the ground and prevented from getting up.

Later on – when the foal is between 12 and 24 hours old and is safe on its feet – the hand is pressed down on its back, in order to desensitise the animal in advance for the weight of the rider. It will also get used to the pressure of the girth. Then the area in which the rider's lower leg will be applied to the horse is sensitised. Again, a stimulus is applied to the appropriate area on the foal and it is permitted to move away from this touch. As soon as the foal reacts, the trainer rewards it by releasing the pressure immediately. By so doing, the foal learns that the pressure will stop whenever it moves away from it. Soon the animal will move away at the lightest touch.

Sensitising can also take place by applying pressure to the chest (for walking backwards) and the hindquarters (to direct the horse forwards), as well as the poll (for halter-breaking, explained later in this book).

JUSTIFIED MANIPULATION?

In this chapter I have deliberately not gone into great detail in explaining the special techniques of desensitisation and sensitisation. I am of the opinion that these procedures are exaggerated for the newly born foal and therefore do not fit into this concept of educating a foal. It is enough to get the foal used to the touch of the human by, for example, drying off the foal with straw or by simply stroking the animal lovingly. The additional (less intense) imprinting on humans takes place automatically during such actions, in such a way that the foal has no

fear of humans. Any techniques such as holding the foal to the ground and preventing it from getting up are forceful measures which may encourage the dependence and subordination of the little individual but at the same time demonstrate clear parallels to "breaking in" which hinders the free development of the psyche – the self-confidence and strength of character. This type of imprint training inhibits the horse's independence, creativity and freedom of choice. It is not possible to educate a partner or friend through this extreme form of imprint training, because the foal is already being manipulated in advance as a "push-button horse". The techniques of Robert Miller may certainly produce good-natured and obliging horses, but a consistent and expert schooling and training during adolescence will produce the same effect. In addition, ensuring that a horse receives excellent schooling means that you will have an animal with a strong character and love of life. Such an animal is a "complete horse", because it was permitted to grow up as such. Imprinting the foal too intensively (or indeed only) on humans, or excessive imprint training, whereby the foal has fingers stuck up all its orifices until it is exhausted, kills the horse's spirit. The horse is no longer itself if it is being manipulated in this manner. True horse lovers, on the other hand, want a horse with all its faults and weaknesses (which should be accepted as natural characteristics in the same way as positive features are), and not a pre-programmed riding-puppet.

FIRST LEARNING STEPS FOR THE FOAL

Using a toned-down version of imprinting on humans has advantages for the horse owner as well as the young foal. A mild form of imprinting includes an added imprinting on the human being, as well as the far stronger bonding with the foal's dam. Imprinting begins immediately at birth, but does not end abruptly. All individuals are blessed with an increased ability to learn things, particularly in the first few weeks of their life, which ensures amongst other things that wild animals will survive. If animals did not learn required behaviour within the shortest time possible, many would not survive. This phase of an increased ability to learn also forms part of the imprinting phase. In the same way that a foal born in the wild learns important rules of behaviour within the herd so that it can cope with life, there are certain stages of learning which the domesticated horse needs which are by all means suitable.

The shy foal gains more trust when the human being crouches down, because he/she no longer appears so large.

The youngster should be taken through these important steps of learning which will ensure that its life with humans is free from fear, trusting, and above all, safe, during the first few days and weeks of its life. The aim of this training, which should be carried out as playfully as possible (in the same manner as you would deal with children), is to take away any fear of humans the foal may harbour. It should allow humans to touch it, stroke it, groom it and administer medication, as well as to lead it with a headcollar.

TOUCHING AND BEING GROOMED

If you are present at the birth of the foal, you can help the mother dry off the new arrival. To do this, take a wisp of straw and dry off the wet coat of the foal. You may only do this task, however, if the mare permits it. In the case of a companionable mare, it usually presents no problems. This is the first step to overcoming the foal's inborn fear of humans. In this instance, exploiting the imprinting phase is appropriate. The foal will show no trace of shyness if touched by humans, thus making future schooling and training a lot easier.

Over the next days and weeks the trainer should continue to handle the foal frequently and regularly. This process includes touching the foal on all body parts, switching to a soft body brush after a certain period, with which to stroke the youngster. Naturally, as long as the trainer is working with the foal, the mare must remain nearby constantly so that it feels safe and secure. Therefore, it makes sense either to tie up the mare or to have an assistant hold her.

If the foal's first contact with humans did not occur immediately following the birth, but instead days later, a certain fear of the humans may already have developed. In this case it would be inappropriate, for example, to push the young foal into a corner in order to be able to touch it. This would only trigger a panic reaction and sow the seeds of mistrust. Far better to use the foal's natural curiosity and to wait patiently until the youngster approaches the trainer of its own free will. While waiting for the youngster to approach, it is better to adopt a crouching position so that the foal does not feel threatened. Therefore, kneel down and speak quietly to the foal. It will soon make a tentative approach in order to sniff curiously at the stranger. Once the youngster has stretched out its head, do not immediately attempt to hold it or stroke it. It is far better to give the animal more time, until it feels more secure and accepts any movements of your hands without fear. Only after the foal has sniffed your hands extensively and does not back off, should you carefully try to stroke its neck and chest. Eventually, you can rub the foal's withers, a thing all youngsters particularly enjoy. In this way you will soon gain the trust of the animal.

As soon as touching the neck and withers no longer presents any problems, the trainer can advance a stage further by carefully touching the entire body of the foal. It is of particular importance not to forget the legs, However, do

This Lusitano filly, which is only a few weeks old, gets to know the body brush. At first, it is allowed to sniff it to convince itself that the object is not dangerous.

As soon as touching the neck and body no longer presents any problems, the trainer can advance a stage further by carefully stroking the legs, Naturally, the dam must be present at all times during training sessions with the foal.

not attempt to hold onto the legs. At this early stage, the foal could become afraid, run away, and refuse to have its legs touched in the future. To make sure the foal becomes tame to touch, only perform actions which do not cause the youngster to flee.

Once the foal allows the trainer to stroke it gently all over, a soft body brush can be used as well. This ensures that the foal becomes used to being groomed, but most importantly and primarily it strengthens the bond between the foal and man. In addition, grooming and massaging stimulates the circulation, which increases the horse's feeling of well-being and contributes to its health.

The shy foal will gain trust more quickly if the trainer crouches down. In the upright position a human comes across as very large and, therefore, a threat to the youngster.

FITTING THE HEADCOLLAR

Apart from being touched, the most important lessons which a young foal must learn as early as possible, are the fitting of a headcollar, being led, and letting you pick up its feet. These lessons are necessary to facilitate future medical treatment of the foal. It needs to be inoculated and wormed without using force.

Having the headcollar fitted is one of the first things which must be learned to keep the foal under control.

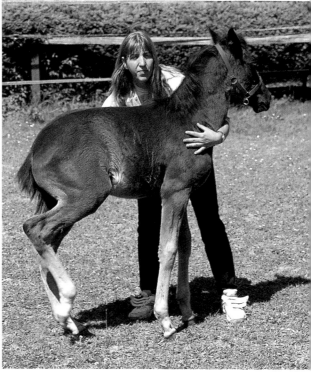

Until the foal is halter-broken, it can be controlled very well by putting your arms around the chest and hindquarters.

This would frighten the foal and have a lasting effect. It would not be possible, for example, to care for an injured foal which will not allow itself to be caught, held, have the headcollar put on, and touched. Failure to accustom foals to these things at an early stage, has cost some youngsters their lives. If the horse lets itself be touched, it is possible to put both arms around its chest and hindquarters, thereby holding it under control. This is still possible with very young foals and can be used as long as the foal has not been halter-broken. But

even the smallest foals often know how strong they are and with a bit of courage can escape from the clinch very quickly – especially if the vet is approaching with a syringe, or a very painful injury needs disinfecting.

Fitting the headcollar is therefore the first step towards leading and halter control. Foals accustomed to touch usually don't have much of a problem when the horse owner pulls a headcollar over its head, especially if they have been accustomed to a brush and other "routine" items. There is no reason for not getting the foal accustomed to tarpaulins, buckets, plastic bags and ropes at this stage. However, during the daily handling of the horses, a dedicated familiarisation training is not necessary as this usually happens automatically in the course of time and the desensitisation process is carried out far more easily this way.

It is more important to concentrate on familiarising the foal with headcollar and lead-rope. A necessary investment is a robust foal headcollar which is adjustable in size. Once the foal allows itself to be touched and stroked without fear, putting the headcollar on and fastening it should present no problems. First, however, the foal should have the opportunity to sniff the headcollar extensively, in order to convince itself of its harmlessness. Then the headcollar is slowly slipped over the nose and the buckle closed on the throat-band.

The foal may now try to shake or rub off the fitted headcollar, therefore it is very important that the foal is under constant supervision when it is wearing its headcollar. If the young foal gets caught on something the consequences could be fatal. For this reason, it is also important never to fit the headcollar too loosely. Should the foal scratch its head with a hindleg it could easily get caught in the loose headcollar. Naturally, the headcollar should not be fitted too tightly either, as this could cause distress to the animal, or even injuries from the pressure.

A basic rule is that the headcollar must never be worn without supervision. This means that the headcollar is never worn in the stable or field, but only when the trainer is working with the animal. In addition, frequent fitting and removal of the headcollar contributes to the familiarisation process.

PICKING UP ITS FEET

As soon as the young horse is steady on its long legs the trainer should start picking up its feet. This is not only necessary for daily hoof care, but also so that the farrier can check, trim and possibly even correct the hooves every now and then. In particular, in cases where the hoofs are deformed or deviate from the correct line, the farrier may have to undertake corrective farriery at a very early age to ensure that the problem is corrected and does not become worse.

Of course the foal must already be used to being touched everywhere in order to be able to pick up its feet correctly. In addition, the youngster should also be used to wearing a headcollar. It is useful to have an assistant to hand, who will hold the foal by its headcollar. Start by touching the little foal all over its body and stroking it lovingly. For this purpose, it is sensible to crouch down so that the youngster gains trust. Once the animal is quiet and enjoys the procedure, you then stroke right down its leg to the fetlock joint. It is advisable to start with a fore leg which, as we know, is easier to pick up than a back leg. Before attempting to pick up the leg, the foal has to transfer its weight to its other three legs, which at this moment is probably the hardest part of the whole process. The trainer can help the foal with this by gently leaning his shoulder against that of the horse. In this way, the animal takes the weight off the corresponding leg and the trainer can lift the hoof from the ground, It is important at this stage to praise the foal extensively and place the hoof back on the ground after a short period in order not the frighten the animal. The whole procedure is repeated a few times, until the foal shows no more signs of insecurity.

Once the hoof has been picked up the next step is to slowly release the pressure on the shoulder. This will teach the animal to balance itself on three legs. If the shoulder were to remain in place as support, the little horse would never learn to spread its weight on its own legs. A horse which has not been trained correctly to do this will present difficulties later in being handled, because it will always transfer some of its weight to the picked-up foot or lean against the person holding the hoof. This can make picking up the feet a nightmare for the horse owner.

If the support is removed early enough, the horse learns to balance itself on its own. When picking up the feet, it is of particular importance not to hold on to the fetlock joint too tightly or to pull the leg away sideways. Both actions are unpleasant for the horse and can lead to the youngster trying to pull its leg away. Also, do not attempt to pull the hoof under the foal's stomach or to bend the joints too severely. This can put undue stress on the joints, in particular the fetlock joint and the knee (carpal) joint, possibly leading to over-stretched ligaments and other injuries. As the foal is still growing, the bone and ligament structures are very soft and vulnerable, there-fore careful handling is recommended to avoid overstretching. Always ensure that the cannon bone is not lifted any higher than a position

After initial insecurity this Paint Horse foal very soon leans to trust its trainer and finally allows its hoof to be lifted without resistance.

The foal must learn to balance its weight on the other three legs when one of its legs is picked up.

Make sure that the hoof of the rear legs is lifted up in a straight line to prevent the fetlock joint from being twisted. Pulling the leg out sideways would again lead to stress in the fetlock joint, the hock and the hip joint.

When placing the hoof back on the ground, it is particularly important to lower gently. If you simply let go of the leg, as is unfortunately often the case, the hoof could hit the ground hard which causes great pain. In the worst case scenario this could lead to a fracture of the coffin bone. If the horse is accustomed to the owner simply letting go of its legs, it will expect this but will therefore keep an increased muscle tone in order to catch the hoof before it hits the ground. This leads to muscle tension and a feeling of unpleasantness. Horses spoilt in this way are more likely to pull away during shoeing or picking out of the hooves and are likely to refuse to stand still.

horizontal to the ground and that the knee joint shows an angle of approximately 90 degrees. Once lifting one leg has been accomplished with success, the same procedure should be used to pick up the other three feet.

THE FIRST ATTEMPTS AT LEADING

If the horse is used to the headcollar at this stage and seems to let the trainer handle without a problem, the time has come for halter-breaking. For this purpose, a strong lead-rope is attached to the headcollar. The leading lesson is one of the most important in the life of a horse, because it is a task the horse is expected to perform every day of its life, and because it is one of the key tasks in making

During the first few attempts at leading the foal, the mare is used as a magnet.

the handling of the horse easy in the future.

The horse must learn to follow humans trustingly and obediently on the lead-rope. The foundations for this have already been laid by accustoming the young foal to be touched and to have a headcollar fitted. With these pre-requisites it should be no problem to teach the foal to be led. The easiest way is to initially use the dam as a "magnet", in order to teach the foal what you want it to do. Therefore an assistant who will lead the dam, would be of an advantage. The foal will be eager to follow its mother. By initially using this inborn urge you can now move the foal in

the direction you want it to go. The person leading the foal should grasp the lead rein about eight inches below the headcollar fitting. The end of the lead-rope is taken up by the other hand. Beware! Even when leading a foal, it is important never to wind the rope around the hand. If the animal is startled and tries to pull away, it is better to let go of the rope than be dragged along the tarmac. Even foals are stronger than humans and are quite capable of doing such a thing. A suckling will never run very far anyway, but will stay near its mother. Nevertheless, leading lessons should always take place in a fenced-off area in which

The person leading the foal has to be able to handle the headcollar and rope responsibly.

If the foal is not acquainted with being led on the lead-rope or if it feels insecure, the trainer can assist it by pushing it forward with his hand placed on its thigh.

mother and foal feel secure and have as few distractions as possible. This is the only way to work quietly and with care in a trusting atmosphere, and thereby minimise the possibility of accidents.

The person leading the mare walks on a few metres ahead and the person leading the foal also starts moving, following the mother. Some foals will follow straightaway, others however stop as if rooted to the ground and merely whinny for their mother but refuse to lead on. If this is the case, the person leading the mare must ensure that he/she does not move too far away, in order not to frighten the foal. Pulling at the lead-rope is not the correct way to induce the foal to move forwards. Instead, the trainer should place one hand on the thigh of the foal and gently push it forward. This encourages most foals to move forward.

If the foal jumps away in high spirits, let the lead-rope run to its full length and try not to exert too much pull on the foal's head, but rather try to bring the boisterous foal under control gently. Overly abrupt pressure, especially on the foal's poll, can have negative consequences. The bone structure of the youngster is still very soft and the poll region in particular has a number of sensitive nerves running along it which could be damaged. This is why certain trainers condemn leading lessons of horses at this early age. However, I think that responsible handling of the headcollar and rope will not cause any damage. However, very young foals should not be tied up at this age, in order to prevent this type of injury. Pulling hard on the rope is another no-no, to eliminate the occurrence of any unpleasant experience or injury.

> The foal trainer must deal with the headcollar and lead-rope in a responsible manner, in order to eliminate the occurrence of injuries and unpleasant experiences for the foal.

The foal will understand the hand pushing it forward on its thigh better than it will a pull on the lead-rope. Soon it will learn that a gentle tug on the rope means that it should follow its leader. A little patience is needed, as the foal is fixated primarily on its mother and initially notices humans only superficially. This means that it isn't yet fully concentrating on the person leading it. Therefore, not obeying the first request has nothing to do with any unwillingness on part of the foal but rather with lack of understanding and/or concentration.

Of course, it is necessary to gain the foal's attention so that it will actually be able to hear the commands, but care should be taken not to overdo things. In any case, at this stage the foal can only concentrate for a few minutes. Also, it is of great importance that the youngster does not lose contact with its mother. Therefore, you should only demand the

attention of the young horse while the mare is close by and the foal can see her at all times. Only after the young foal is reassured that its mother is nearby will it be prepared to transfer its attention to the human trainer.

Frequent verbal repetitions and gentle signals with the lead-rope will encourage the foal to start following the trainer step by step. It won't be long before the animal understands what it is supposed to do. Even once the "all legs" little horse leads well from the lead-rope, never consider taking it too far away from its mother. It is important to avoid uncertainties even while teaching the foal to be led. The foal receives its feeling of security primarily from its mother.

Special care is advised if the foal tends to jump away forward. If the urge to move forward is halted too abruptly with the lead-rope, the youngster will throw up its head and will often rear on this occasion. This presents a real danger that the foal will fall over backwards. Such a traumatic experience, which can also all too easily lead to injury, should always be avoided.

In the event that even after sustained efforts the foal fails to understand that it should be following the lead-rope, the trainer can try using the "Come-Along-Rope".

For this purpose, a sufficiently long lead-rope or a second separate lead-rope is crossed over the foal's back and passed under the tail to lie over the foal's thighs (figure of eight). This method is also suitable for older foals, which are already so big that it is difficult to put your hands around them. The second lead-rope applies gentle pressure and will encourage the young animal to move forwards. A pre-requisite of this type of lead-rope training is that the horse permits the trainer to touch it all over and will accept the lead-rope around its hindquarters without resistance. If the foal becomes restless or afraid, however, it should initially be adequately desensitised to all forms of touching before using the "Come-Along-Rope".

LEARNING WITH MOTHER

The bond between foal and mother prevents the trainer from carrying out a number of activities with the foal and these will have to be postponed until later. However, it is not necessary to undertake too much during the suckling period. The period after weaning is often far better suited to carrying out these tasks. The pain of the foal's separation from its mother after weaning may be alleviated by means of a multitude of activities and the opportunity may be used to strengthen your own bond with the youngster. The art of successful raising and schooling of a foal lies in teaching the right lessons at the right time.

The first six to nine months during which the foal is fed by its dam is a suitable time for lessons during which a second horse is used as an example or lead horse to teach the untrained animal certain tasks more quickly and with greater ease. The best lead for the foal is of course its dam. The strong bond with the mare is used in the following lessons to enable the foal to learn playfully. There is no simpler way to teach a horse.

WALKING ON THE LEAD-ROPE ATTACHED TO A SURCINGLE

A very good form of lead-rope training is that of attaching the foal to the mother. For this purpose, a special surcingle is strapped around the dam, to which the foal is then tied. The lead-rope training described above should have been carried out in advance, so that the foal knows the basics and willingly runs alongside. If the foal is "thrown in at the deep end" and tied to the surcingle without any preparation, it may well object violently and rear up or pull on the lead-rope in a panic. This can lead to falls and injuries. Even being near the mother will not calm the foal in a situation like this.

If you wish to take a youngster to a show, you have to ensure in any case that the foal leads from the surcingle, because the organisers usually demand this form of presentation of the foal. On these occasions, a foal which does not pull on the lead-rope, jump forward, or brace its legs against the ground, will leave the better impression. If the foal is led from the surcingle more frequently it will become increasingly safer. The proximity of its mother gives the youngster additional security and the foal will submit very quickly and will soon enjoy running along beside its mother on the lead-rope.

Tying the foal to the surcingle of the dam is also quite useful when taking mother and foal for a walk, especially if there is no assistant at hand to lead mother or foal separately. This method accustoms the foal to conditions on roads and paths. In addition, it is also a special experience for the young foal, if it gets to know the dangers of the countryside at an early stage. As the imprinting stage lasts a few weeks, getting the youngster used to traffic at this stage can be a valuable contribution to training a horse which will be safe later in life.

When tying the foal to the mother, it is essential, of course, that she herself is completely safe on the roads and across country. One leap sideways by the mother could endanger the foal as well as the person leading. In addition, the foal would simply learn to fear those things which the mother spooks at, such as traffic or other objects.

Usually the foal is tied to the right hand (off) side of the surcingle. In order to ensure that the foal has a balanced training, which will be of an advantage in its later years as a riding horse, the youngster should also become accustomed to being led from the off side. It is therefore practical to occasionally let the youngster run along on the near side of its dam. Naturally, the mare is led from the off side for this purpose. It is necessary for the mother to be accustomed to being led from the off side. Be careful, however! Never practise this lead-rope training unless the mare is happy in traffic! As horses are always led on

Tying the foal to the mother is an excellent lead-rope training. After initial hesitation, the foal soon follows willingly alongside its mother.

the right hand side of the road (unlike the ridden horse, which must be ridden on the left side of the road), they need to be protected from the traffic. Thus, the person leading the horse will always walk between the horse and the traffic. Therefore, the foal which is tied to the surcingle will always walk on its mother's off side. In this way, it is shielded from the road traffic by the mare.

In traffic, the foal is always shielded from the road traffic.

A few safety measures need to be observed when tying the foal to the mother's surcingle. For one thing, the lead-rope should be neither too long nor too short. If the lead-rope is too long, the foal could lower its head to the ground and get its front feet entangled in the lead-rope. This will inevitably cause a panic reaction and maybe a fall resulting in injuries. If, on the other hand, the lead-rope is too short the foal will be put under stress from the constant pressure on its poll. This can cause physical damage as well as psychological stress. Adequate freedom of movement is therefore important.

It goes without saying that all materials being used must be free of faulty craftsmanship or wear and tear. If the ring on the surcingle is torn off, or if the foal's headcollar snaps due to wear and the foal is unexpectedly let loose, this could result in a life-threatening

situation (e.g. in road traffic). Therefore one should always double check tack and equipment when handling horses. This is especially important if you have two horses to keep under control.

FIRST EXPERIENCES "OUT AND ABOUT"

Once the foal follows well on the lead-rope and tied to its mother, the next step will be to make excursions out and about. It makes sense to accustom the foal at an early age to the conditions on roads and in the countryside. As mentioned before, the foal will learn this lesson without much effort if it is running beside its mother, and the countryside holds many surprises and challenges in store which the horse will be confronted with throughout its life. The safety of the rider depends on the horse's ability to deal with these challenges.

During the first few excursions, care should be taken not to stay out too long, as the youngster, despite showing a great amount of enthusiasm and high spirits, will soon tire and will require rest in the form of an undisturbed nap. A walk of 15 to 20 minutes is more than adequate to start off with.

Experience has shown that if the foal is not tied to the surcingle but led by the trainer while an assistant is in charge of the mare, it is better for the foal to follow behind its dam. This, however, can be a problem in road traffic. If the foal is unsettled by traffic approach-

When going on excursions into the countryside, take into account that foals become tired quickly and will need a break. Therefore, the first few excursions should be limited to about 20 minutes.

ing from behind, it would be better to lead the pair next to each other, although this may mean that the entire lane is blocked. The safety of man and beast, however, must have the highest priority.

Out in the open, it is important that the foal can see its mother clearly all the time during the leading session. In woods or in an open field you can also let the foal run free next to its mother, as long as there are no dangers such as road traffic, hidden ditches or similar things nearby. The foal will take this opportunity to start exploring his surroundings. It will sniff curiously at flowers along the way, nibble at a tuft of grass here and there, and inspect a hidden ditch with a great deal of

The youngster soon learns the dangers of the countryside at its mother's side. Once the owner starts hacking the mare out again a few weeks after the birth, this is a good opportunity to take the foal along on the lead-rein.

excitement. However, during all this it will never lose sight of its mother. If you can repeat the adventure of a "hack out and about" as often as possible, the youngster will become increasingly confident and will increase the distance from its mother more and more.

During this stage it is particularly important to keep the foal in sight at all times. One slight lapse of attention on the part of the foal while you are moving out of sight around a corner with its dam, and the eye contact is lost. Suddenly, the foal will feel alone, will start whinnying in panic for its mother and will rush around in an agitated manner. This traumatic experience can have a lasting effect on the foal and disrupt its development towards more independence. In later life, you could end up with a horse which refuses to leave its companions. It is quite normal for the foal to lag back up to 100 metres while it is examining interesting objects. Once its curiosity has been satisfied, it will gallop after its mother and probably overtake her to gain a lead which will give it time to look at other new objects. The more temperamental the young foal, the more impetuously it will behave in the open. This can be dangerous and can lead to injuries due to the foal's inattention; therefore it is really important only to let the foal off the lead in completely danger-free areas.

A few weeks after the birth the mare can be ridden again. If, in the meantime, the foal has learned to follow on the lead-rope or attached to the surcingle, there will be no problem in taking the foal out hacking on the lead-rein. Frequent handling and the lead-rope training the foal has so far experienced will mean that the foal will have learned to trust humans sufficiently. If its relationship with the owner is good, the foal can now run along beside the mare without a lead when hacking out. If the rider approaches a road or any other danger spot, a call is often sufficient for the foal to

If the foal runs along with the mare off the lead in danger-free countryside, it will go on journeys of discovery and enjoy romping about. In this situation, excessive high spirits can sometimes lead to the foal losing its footing and landing on its nose – as seen here.

It is great fun to observe the foal coping with the unknown element water!

drink from its mother approximately every ten minutes. It goes without saying that you must let the foal have its way and interrupt the hack for the duration.

If the foal has been taught to lead off the surcingle strapped around its mother, it can now be tied to the ring of the breast plate or the horn of the western saddle when the dam is being ridden under the saddle. In the event that the rider wishes to trot or canter, it is better that the foal's lead-rope is held by the hand. If the foal stumbles or jumps away in high spirits, the restriction placed on its freedom of movement could mean a nasty fall. If it is tied to the saddle serious injuries could occur.

Similarly, it is not practical to tie the foal to the saddle in difficult situations. If you want to cross a stream and the foal is afraid of stepping into the water, as it is an unknown quantity for it, dragging it by force into the water could cause a trauma. Instead, the rider should make use of the bond with its mother and ride ahead with the mare. Once the mare has crossed the stream you must not simply ride on but rather must wait patiently until the foal overcomes its fear and follows on. Depending on the situation, it may even be better to remain in the water. Take into account, however, that the foal is likely to suddenly plunge into the stream and make for its dam. It is great fun to observe the foal coping with water as an element. It may stamp its hooves or snort at the wet element, causing the water to ripple. This could frighten the foal, causing it to leap into the air on all fours.

come back for the lead-rope to be reattached. With a well-trained foal, having to dismount, running after the foal, and drawn-out attempts at catching it will not be necessary.

The horse owner should not forget that, during a walk or hack, the foal will want to

The Arab foal "Silver Diamond" is learning how to cope with outdoor situations with playful intrigue and without the trainer having to resort to force.

Crossing bridges and other obstacles in the countryside should become a matter of course for the foal.

This playful learning process is the best preparation for the demands it will later face as a riding horse.

The trainer needs to be just as patient when the foal is learning to cross bridges or other obstacles in the countryside. Never use violence and force the foal over an obstacle with a whip or by dragging it across on the leadrope. Schooling and training should be based on the principles of trust and should involve as little force as possible. Moreover, the foal has three years at least, to learn to cope with these conditions before it faces the serious life of a riding horse. During this time the foal should be brought up as a "horse-child" and allowed to approach everything with child-like curiosity.

TRAVELLING IN THE HORSE BOX

Excursions into the countryside do not spell the end of learning with mother. Attending different shows can also enrich the life of a foal, as long as the hectic activity usual at such events is not transferred to the youngsters. It may be sensible not to visit a horse show as a first outing as show classes can cause a great deal of stress for rider and horse. Taking a foal along in such a situation invariably increases the stress levels of the rider as well as those of the dam. This, in turn, will be transmitted directly to the psyche of the foal. The result will be that the foal will always associate horse shows with stress: a negative experience which should be avoided at all costs.

Attending a horse show is acceptable provided the rider and the owner of the dam don't attend with the sole aim of winning, but rather put the interests of the foal first. For this purpose, it is quite sufficient just to ride the mare in the collecting ring without actually riding in a class. The foal cannot differentiate between its dam competing or not. The stress level on the other hand can be reduced considerably.

The foal should learn through play and therefore it is advisable to undertake trips for the sake of pure pleasure. Many events are suitable for this purpose, for example charity rides and small gymkhanas with demonstrations and mounted games. Quite apart from the fact that taking the foal along is a new and interesting experience for the horse owner, the mother and foal are sure to catch the eyes of other riders and spectators. Without doubt, the foal will be the darling of every event, which is always a bonus.

In some countries it is necessary to load the mare and foal into a horse box or trailer to take it to a showing class, where the foal is branded and receives its papers.

A basic requirement for visiting horse shows is the loading of mare and foal into a horse box or trailer, as well as the trip itself. Therefore, this is one of the first items on the training schedule of a foal. It makes no sense to take the foal to a show the first time it has been loaded, as the youngster will have to cope with too many new things at once. Such an action will cause stress and insecurity, which is not a good introduction for a young horse to such events. That is why the trainer should approach the lesson step by step. Teaching the foal to load into a trailer or horsebox is one of the most important things it will have to learn, as this could become a matter of life or death under certain circumstances. In case of a colic which needs operating on (twisted gut), safe and efficient loading is a must, if you don't want to waste precious time.

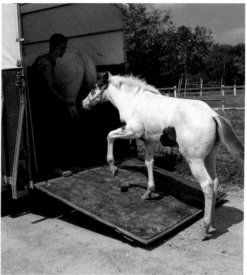

The necessity of transporting a mare and foal by trailer or horsebox may occur quite early in the foal's life. Therefore, loading lessons are a very important item on the agenda. At its first loading lesson, the trainer must show plenty of patience until the foal has the courage to follow its mother into the trailer.

A trainer should make use of the time during which the foal follows the mare at foot, by teaching the foal to load, which should hap-

Teaching the foal to load into a trailer or horsebox is one of the most important lessons it will have to learn.

pen almost automatically when the dam is there. One pre-requisite, of course, is that the dam loads without any fuss herself.

The trailer is prepared in advance by removing the partition in order to create as much space as possible for mother and foal. There is a very large variety of horse trailers, which are more or less suitable for transporting a mare and foal. Attention should be given to specific aspects in order to transport mother and child safely.

Basic requirements for a trailer are a bright interior, a long and low ramp, non-slip floor and, in principle, an injury-proof construction. There are further aspects to take into consideration for transporting a mare with foal, which not every trailer offers. As the partition in a two-horse trailer must be removed, the front and rear bars will have to be removed as well. However, there are trailers which have a front bar which runs the entire width of the trailer and which can remain in the horsebox despite removing the partition. It affords the mare the necessary support during a braking manoeuvre. A second aspect that needs to be considered when transporting foals, is the security of the rear opening above the closed ramp. Depending on which type of trailer is used, it needs to be closed - by tarpaulin or flap - thus preventing the foal, which is never tied up during transport, from jumping out over the ramp. As the air cannot circulate in trailers which are sealed on all sides and it can become stuffy very quickly, a special foal-guard made from sturdy mesh should be used instead, thus letting air in and securing the way out at the same time. This foal-guard or closing the rear opening with a flap or tarpaulin is essential as there have been several instances where foals have jumped out of the trailer at the rear onto the road. The consequences of this do not need spelling out.

If all safety equipment is fitted, the adventure of travelling in a trailer can be undertaken.

To begin with, you should load the foal safely together with its mother. This requires at least one assistant, who leads the mare into the trailer. The foal follows its mother on the lead-rope. If the youngster follows up the ramp behind its mother and into the trailer without hesitation you are lucky. In most cases the foal becomes rooted to the ground in front of the ramp and stares nonplussed into the dark hole of the trailer. It sees no reason for stepping on the ramp of the trailer. Seeing that its mother is not going anywhere, the foal reckons that its position in front of the ramp is quite in order.

This is when the foal handler will prove his or her worth. At this stage he/she should already have a trusting relationship with the foal. There is little sense in pulling on the lead-rope, because even foals are far stronger than humans. Patience, gentle verbal persuasion and light nudging around the thighs of the foal usually have the best results in coaxing the youngster to step onto the ramp. Often, the thudding noise its hooves make on the ramp will spook the foal. This is often the only reason why it refuses to step onto the ramp. Leading the young foal over wooden boards on the ground can be a good preparation for loading training.

Since well-trained foals will let you pick up their feet without any resistance, picking up the front leg and placing it on the ramp can help in this case. Step by step, the petrified youngster will move forwards and up, until all four feet are planted firmly on the ramp. Soon it will realise that this takes it nearer to its dam and it will generally take the remaining steps into the trailer on its own.

On the other hand, it can happen that the foal resists strongly and jumps off the ramp on all fours, or even tries to rear. If this is the case you need to proceed with even more care and patience. Above all, do not force the foal! Basito drive the foal forwards with whip or lead it away from the ramp to make a new approach. The whip causes too much pressure and force for the youngster, which it cannot cope with and which may well lead to psychological problems. Leading the foal away from the ramp also means leading it away from its mother. This isn't the answer either. The best idea is simply to let the foal stand in front of the ramp. At some point, natural curiosity wins over and the youngster makes its first move forward. Naturally, it is permitted to sniff the loading ramp, to reassure itself that it presents no danger.

As soon as the foal has entered the trailer, it is allowed to leave it again with its mother. It is recommended that the ramp be raised and closed only once the foal has learned to follow its mother into the trailer without hesitation. This is usually only the case after a few tries. The mother is tied up in the trailer while the foal is free to come and go. By removing the partition, the foal has sufficient space to move around so that it will find the best place to stand during the trip and can also reach its mother's udder. If loading up and raising the ramp have become routine, the journey can commence at last. It should be unnecessary to mention how important it is to drive particularly carefully. Remember that with the partition removed the mare has no side support to keep her balance with. The foal too will encounter problems with balance because, due to its long legs, its centre of gravity is very high. In addition, travelling in a trailer or horsebox is a completely new situation for the

Loading is a lesson which the foal can learn superbly at its mother's side.

cally, the foal does want to walk into the trailer, because it wants to be near its mother. But it needs time to evaluate the situation and overcome its fears. It would be equally unwise

youngster which is sure to unsettle it. On the other hand, the mother will provide the necessary reassurance and soon the foal will become accustomed to the situation.

The first journey should last no longer than about five to ten minutes, in other words, just round the block. With time, increase the duration of the journey until it becomes routine and a more distant destination can be headed for.

THE FIRST INDEPENDENT ADVENTURES

The first six months are altogether one of the most rewarding phases for the foal owner. As long as the foal is so small and dependent on the mother it is great fun to handle it and observe it playing in the field every day. You should enjoy this phase and use it for doing activities together. This period is the best opportunity you will have to teach the foal the things it has to learn in a playful way. Of course, the well-being of the mare must be taken into account at all times during these enterprises. She will always worry about her foal, which leads to psychological stress, and she will also be subject to physical strain due to the fact that she is producing milk. Therefore, the care of the mare must not be forgotten; the owner must be fully aware of the fact that he/she now has two horses to look after.

At some point, however, mare and foal will have to be separated. The weaning process represents a radical new step in the life of dam and foal And the foal needs to be prepared accordingly. Preparations start as early as three or four months into the foal's life when it will take its first independent steps in the care of its owner/trainer.

GOING IT ALONE

Once the foal is a few months old, you will find that it increases the distance it strays from its mother further and further and that in the field it no longer remains constantly beside its dam. It will start showing an interest in the foals of other mares, it will play

The first independent enterprises prepare the foal for the weaning process.

with them, and spend its time taking part in races and play-fighting. Only when it becomes thirsty and needs to rest will it turn to its mother for milk and protection. It will also seek refuge near its mother if any strange things happen which cause it to feel insecurity or even fear: for example, a combine harvester passing along outside the field.

The foal is now old enough to venture out alone in the company of its familiar owner. In order to encourage the youngster's independence, the trainer can begin by leading it away from its mother on the lead-rope. Initially, you should make sure that the foal remains in constant eye contact with its mother. Once the foal feels more secure, you may lead it out of sight around a corner. These excursions can slowly be extended, depending on how confident the foal feels.

REMAINING ALONE

If the owner has taken enough time to handle the foal, it will trust him accordingly. Separated from its mother, it can still gain reassurance from the human being it trusts. It is an entirely different matter if the youngster has to remain on its own. The foal will not be spared this experience, for one day the time will come when the mare is taken out of the field in order to separate her from the foal, initially for a short time.

To make the pain of the separation bearable, the foal should naturally be with other horses. The least painful separation from the mother occurs if the foal remains within its familiar herd, where it can play with other foals. At the same time make sure that the field is escape-proof, because some foals will go to extreme lengths to follow their mothers and ignore any kind of barrier, which could lead to serious injuries. I once witnessed this situation

The older it gets, the more the foal will try out things on its own.

When in doubt, the foal will still seek security at its mother's side.

with an Arab foal, which succeeded in jumping through the horizontal wooden bars of a fence. Another foal even decided to jump over a four-foot-six high wooden fence so as not be left behind by its mother as she was being led out of the paddock on her own. The foal landed on a mountain of roof tiles, wooden boards and other rubbish, which had been piled up behind the fence. Fortunately the youngster only suffered grazes, which soon healed.

Therefore, great attention must be paid to ensuring that the foal is left behind in a secure environment when being separated from its mother. If the foal's behaviour indicates that its mother's presence is more important to it than any horses in the field, the youngster will have to be shut away in a closed loose box where there is no escape and in which the danger of injury is minimised. However, at least one horse, which the foal knows, should be placed in the neighbouring box. Each foal will respond differently to the separation, and you will always have to proceed with care and use your common sense in deciding what to do.

If the foal is left alone, whether in the field or in the box, the initial separation should only last for a few minutes. Of course the foal will whinny for its mother at first, but will soon calm down when the dam returns. After a few repeats of this, the foal will respond more calmly to each separation, for it knows that its dam will be back very soon. Once the youngster accepts the mother's short absences and stops responding in a panic, the duration of the separation can be increased. The older the foal, the longer the period of separation

If the foal is separated from its dam for a short time, it should at least be surrounded by other horses from its herd.

can be. In every situation, the trainer must ensure that the foal will get the chance to drink milk when it needs to. Initially, the foal turns to its mother for milk every ten to fifteen minutes. Later on, when its diet is supplemented by hard feed, these intervals increase. Shortly before being weaned, a foal can be left by itself for an hour without a problem. Thus, the mare's function as a riding horse becomes less and less restricted. You should however remember that she requires a large amount of energy for milk production. A mare with a suckling must be fed and treated accordingly (i.e. high levels of protein). A mare with a foal at foot should be spared the dual pressure of being a mother and high performance sports horse.

WEANING THE FOAL

A time comes when the foal is finally separated from the mare. This process is called weaning. Weaning is necessary for two reasons. Firstly, the mare is taxed and tired to a high degree by the very energy expensive process of milk production. In particular, if the mare is in foal again she should be allowed rest to prepare herself for the new foal. Secondly, the foal needs to become independent and learn to go its own way. If the youngster is not weaned expertly the foal "clings" to the mare for many years. This has a negative effect on the further training and schooling of the horse.

Horses who stick to others can (if separated from their partner, the mother in the case of unweaned foals) develop vices which make handling these horses very difficult, and which can also impair the health of the animal. The driving force that governs the horse's instinct to stay near its mother can mean that you end up with a horse that rears, kicks, or bucks.

Lack of attention towards humans is another factor, present in horses which refuse to be separated from others (as their entire attention is fixed on their vanished partner) which can lead to dangerous situations both for humans and animals.

Therefore, weaning is a necessary process which takes place for the good of mare, the foal and also humans. However, the process must be prepared correctly in order not to become a nightmare for foal and dam. At any rate, weaning is an important phase in the life of a foal and must be carried out with due care and attention.

WHEN IS THE RIGHT TIME?

Even experts do not agree about the method or the time when weaning should take place. In principle, circumstances are usually the deciding factor as to when and in which way the weaning process is carried out. The advantages and disadvantages must be weighed against each other, but above all personal circumstances have to be considered.

The method of weaning needs to be well thought out and prepared, so that it does not become a nightmare for the foal.

In theory a foal can survive without its mother's milk from the age of three months. Therefore, horse owners who wish to use the mare for competitions (horse shows or races) usually choose to wean very early since the mare needs to be at her fittest as a sports horse as soon as possible. A foal at foot would simply be a hindrance. It could be argued that it would have been better for a foal which was weaned early for the above reasons never to have been born in the first place. Although it may not suffer physically through being weaned at ten to twelve weeks, the psychological effects could be all the more disastrous. The foal is certainly not independent enough to find its way around without its mother. In such a case, even the most tender care from humans would be of little use. To understand this better an analogy may help. If a one-year-old child were placed in nursery school the child would feel totally lost and scream for its mother. Even five-year-old children are not capable of caring entirely for themselves without the support of their parents. This comparison is certainly inadequate, but there are parallels all the same.

Weaning (from the milk source) at the age of three months is only acceptable if the mother produces too little milk and the foal is always sucking an empty udder. If it has been established that the mother has too little milk, then replacement foal milk is added to the feed. One of the first things is to familiarise the foal with hard feed (foal starter, grain, hay or grass). In addition, you should start to keep the foal away from its dam's udder (gentle

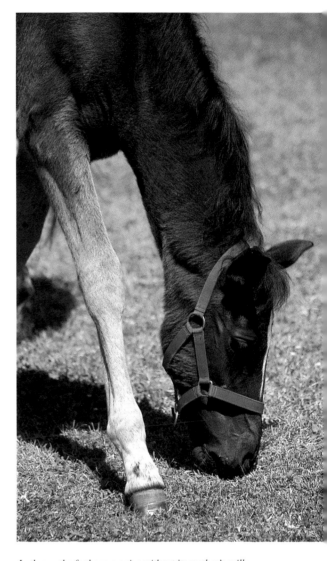

In theory the foal can survive without its mother's milk from an age of three months.

weaning). Feeding the foal with replacement foal milk until it is replete before reuniting mare and foal helps to "dry out" the mare. This means that the foal does not need to be separated completely from its mother but can continue to stay with her, which is very important for its psychological development.

As a rule, mares do not wean their foals off themselves. Although cases have been observed where the dam refuses to let the foal near the udder at approximately one year of age, normally foals suckle for years if the mare does not have another one. In the wild, the mare will chase her foal away as soon as the next foal is born. This is usually the case after one year. Sometimes, if the mare should fail to conceive the previous year, the foal might suckle for two years.

In the care of humans the suckling period of the foal is primarily determined by the intended use of the mare. If the mare is not solely a brood-mare but also a riding horse, early weaning may well suit the owner's wishes. Even a mare which is used only for breeding needs time to gain new strength before the next foal is born. This is also a reason for weaning early.

However, if you breed a single foal from your mare and use the mother only moderately as a riding horse, it does no harm to let the foal stay with its dam for an entire year. After one year, however, even this foal should take its first steps towards independence and be weaned. As the foal should be turned out in the field with other youngsters of its age, it may not always be possible to wean it as a yearling, due to the fact that the others which will have been weaned at an earlier age are sent back out with their mother (i.e. integrated back into the herd at this stage), and the

freshly weaned yearling would have to remain on its own. Therefore, outside circumstances usually determine the method and time of weaning.

If at all possible, foals should be weaned when they are between six and twelve months old. This period can be regarded as the general rule and, although the above mentioned deviations may sometimes be necessary they should by no means be pursued just for the sake of simplicity.

In theory, breeding studs could let the foals be weaned "naturally", as the mares are usually covered directly after birth. However, this is avoided since it has been discovered that mares which suckle last year's foal for too long have less strength for the new-born foal. Experience shows that mares produce the best foals if they are only covered every two years. Early weaning of last year's foal also produces better offspring in the following year. This consideration is particularly important for race horses and sports horses. Some breeders will experience qualms of conscience in view of these findings. These can be resolved if the two-year rota is chosen and the breeding mare is covered only every second year. The (only) factor against this method is that of cost.

ABRUPT WEANING, OR STEP BY STEP?

Each breeder has their own opinions regarding the method of weaning. Again, outside cir-

Usually the outside conditions determine the time of weaning.
If possible, this should not take place before the foal is seven months old.

cumstances play a major role. Many breeders swear that abrupt weaning is best, others prefer slow weaning.

> Foals should be weaned between the age of six and twelve months.

Abrupt weaning means that mare and foal are separated from one day to the next. They must be accommodated out of ear shot and eye contact with each other.

In practice, this is only possible if a horse leaves the yard and is stabled in another yard. Many breeders who sell their foals as soon as they are weaned, choose this option. After six months the new owner collects the foal, which should then be integrated into a herd with others of the same age. This helps the foal overcome the separation from the mother in a new environment. A tip for those who wish to practise this method of weaning, because they intend to sell their foal: it is easier, if the foal is not loaded into the horse box on its own, but travels to the new yard with its dam and is only then separated from her. Loading and transport problems could occur if the foal is moved elsewhere on its own. A traumatic experience of this dimension could lead to future difficulties in loading.

Some mares suffer much more after abrupt weaning because they have to deal with the pain of separation as well as the pressure of the full udder. Especially mares which produce a lot of milk will have problems with a swollen udder. It can lead to inflammation of the udder, a rare occurrence. If this happens, the vet should be called out. However, even if the mare suffers from a swollen udder, it would be completely wrong to milk her. This would only lead to the mare producing even more milk, thus increasing the pressure on the udder. If the foal stops drinking and you don't milk the dam she will cease to produce milk. If the foal is put back to the mother prematurely, it will remember the delicious source of milk and begin suckling again. This can lead to reactivation of milk production. The time it takes until the mare is "dry" can vary greatly. In the case of abrupt weaning it therefore makes sense to separate foal and mother for at least three to six months.

Due to circumstances I weaned my Arab foal abruptly. For this purpose, before weaning took place I got a second foal which had been weaned from its mother and was integrated into our herd. The foals got on well immediately and the new arrival – a beautiful black mare – immediately joined the dam of my Arab foal, so that some visitors even suspected twin foals. After about two weeks of settling in, it was time to wean my Arab foal. The filly was now seven months old and the first snow had fallen. I simply took both foals on a short lead-rope and walked with them across snow-covered fields to the next village, where we were already expected by a friend who ran a livery yard. The foals came along willingly; they had been well prepared for weaning and were familiar with short walks from which their mothers were absent.

The foals were now integrated into a herd of twelve horses, ruled by a large seventeen-hand Irish gelding called "Vinlay". The herd consisted of yearlings, two-year-olds, as well as younger and older riding horses. The breeds too, were a colourful mixture, ranging from a Shetland pony, through a quarter horse, to a warm blood. After a week I received another quarter horse weanling, which also joined the other two other foals. The horses within the mixed herd, which was turned out in a very large field, soon formed groups. We found that three weaned foals – an Arab filly, which was already beginning to turn grey, a black warm-blood mare and a chestnut quarter horse mare – formed a clique and went about everywhere together. The foals received appropriate training from the older horses about how they should behave within the herd. In the "horse nursery" they learned how to be a "horse" the natural way. There was very little time to pine away for mother. Of course, the bond with humans remained since the care of the horse was in my hands. I made sure to continue the further training and schooling of the youngsters and exercises such as picking up of the legs, leading on the headcollar and loading, were carried out almost daily. When called by name, the foals would leave the heard and come galloping up the hill. Although the foals behaved as if they were members of a sworn youth gang, they could be taken out on their own without too much sticking.

The foals stayed together in the herd for six months and then went back to their mothers and their home stables. I was able to follow the fate of the three foals: they all became good, easy-to-handle and reliable mounts.

If the dams suffer visibly after the separation, they should be kept occupied in order to take their mind off things. Mares with a swollen udder should also have a lot of exercise. Long, quiet hacks and gentle schooling help to overcome the pain of separation and soon help the mare to get used to normal, everyday riding once again.

If possible, you should take the opportunity to wean your foal off the mother gradually. This is advisable if you are raising several foals (at least two) and the horses can be accommodated in loose boxes or in separate paddocks as well as out in the pasture. For this method, mare and foal are simply separated during feeding times. The best way to do this is to stable the two foals in one loose box or lock them into a small run where both of the mothers are either stabled in adjoining boxes to the left and right or in a neighbouring paddock. This ensures eye contact at all times, but the foal is separated from its source of milk for a short time.

After some time the separation can be increased over a period of several hours or overnight. This is practical because in many yards the horses are stabled overnight and go out to pasture during the day. Increasingly long periods of separation and good supplementary feeding of the foal result in the mare producing less and less milk. Finally, foal and mare can remain separate and only be reunited once the mare has stopped producing milk.

When weaning is carried out step by step, you should take care to encourage solo excursions to prevent horses from "sticking" to each other. This is difficult, if the separation does not last for months, but there is actually eye and ear contact every day. If slow weaning becomes difficult, mother and child will finally have to be separated completely and stabled out of eye and ear contact. As a result there is a combination of slow and fast weaning, which is the best solution overall.

AFTER WEANING

As the previous example illustrates, playmates of the same age are particularly important for

*Weanlings should become used to solo excursions, in order to ensure
that they will not "stick" to other horses later in life.*

the foal directly after weaning. On the one
hand, they comfort the foal during the pain of
separation and on the other, the youngsters
learn to get on with other members of their
species. In addition, they train their lungs and
muscles during play, play-fighting and racing.
If the weaned foals are integrated into a herd
on their own, they often stand around quite

lost and lonely, despite the other horses, and mourn for their mother. No person can give the necessary comfort in this situation. Many horse owners think that they can help their foals during the period of separation if they care intensively for their foal especially during this phase. This method harbours the danger of humanising the youngster too much. A human being cannot take over the role of a playmate of similar age. Instead, by entering into "foal games" in the field, immense problems can be conjured up. Foals, which rear up and kick can be dangerous even at this stage. Later on, when the foal is half or fully grown, it will be difficult to cure it of the habit of rearing up at or kicking humans. The horse is unable to grasp why it is no longer allowed to play as it was used to doing. If the foal becomes rebellious towards older members of the herd, by rearing up or kicking them, all the older horse needs to do is warn it by laying back its ears, which will put the over-confident foal in its place. If the foal becomes too much of a menace, it might require a nip to put it in its place. Within the herd, foals soon find their place in the order of rank. As a rule, the weanling will be unable to pull rank against the older horses. Therefore, it will have to measure its strength against its contemporaries, for only here is any "victory" possible at all.

Foals which do not have any playmates of a similar age will always be ranked very low in the herd and will not develop self-confidence and courage. As a rule, they will remain mentally and physically underdeveloped.

Of course, older horses within the herd also play an important part in the weanling's life. They raise the youngster and teach it manners. This experience is especially useful for the further development of the horse. But older horses do not make good playmates. They will not join in any games, play-fighting and racing. I once came across a foal which had lived alone in a herd. It constantly tried to persuade a one-and-a-half-year old chestnut mare to play with it. The mare, however, was not impressed and violently fended off the eight-month-old weanling. Not even horses only six or nine months older make ideal playmates for the foal. The principle therefore is that foals must be around the same age. They should at least be born in the same year.

If one foal is two or three months older than another foal there are usually no disadvantages. No doubt, the development of the older foal will be more advanced, so that it will able to battle out a higher rank over the younger foal and definitely have the say in their friendly relationship. On the other hand, the young foal will profit from the experience of its slightly older partner, so that it will develop faster and soon approach the same level of development as its older playmate.

The relationship amongst weanlings can perhaps be compared with the constellation of siblings. If one sibling (brother or sister) is a few years older, the younger sibling will profit immensely from its older sibling's experience and knowledge. On the other hand, the latter will already have other interests. Therefore, for

After weaning, the company of youngsters of a similar age is important, although the precense of older horses too is useful.

us humans, siblings which are only a year younger or older make better playmates.

A human cannot put himself in place of a horse regarding its education of growing up as a horse, so he cannot take the role of a "replacement mother" or playmate of similar age. This must be left to horses which can do it naturally and certainly much better.

On the other hand, humans must take over the training of the young horse to prepare it for its role as riding horse in later life. This sphere of tasks is enormous and very demanding. In this way, the companion horses in the field have their specific tasks just as the human does in ensuring that the weanling

> After being separated from the mother, foals require, in particular, contact with playmates of a similar age.

turns out to be a well-mannered and easily handled horse. The tasks, however, need to be clearly defined and separated.

WEANED FOALS AND YEARLINGS

LESSONS IN THE FIRST AND SECOND YEAR

Once the foal has been separated from its mother, it is referred to as a "weanling". The youngster is called a yearling from 1st January of the year after its birth. In this context, it makes no difference whether the foal was born in March or November of the previous year. Even foals which are born in autumn are called yearlings at the age of two or three months. As a rule, the mares are covered early in the spring so that the foals are born preferably in April or May. Therefore the yearlings will be about three-quarters of a year old the following January but a good year and a-half by November of the same year.

When we talk of yearlings here, we mean foals which have already been weaned and are between at least six to nine months old, independent of 1st January as the qualifying date. The following lessons are thus intended for youngsters which are independent of the mother and at least six to eight months old.

Most horse owners find they can do little with a weanling or yearling. Yet this period of development in the horse's life is especially crucial. But as long as the youngsters cannot be lunged or ridden, their owners are often at a loss about what they could do with their horses. The reason for this is simply that hardly anyone teaches horse owners which lessons can be taught to an as yet unbacked horse. This lack of knowledge often leads to trainers dismissing schooling at this age as "child's play" and to disapprove of it. But do we shut our children in a room and wait until they are old enough to go to school? Or do we prepare them for school and life by playing with them, going to the zoo and showing them the animals, teaching them how to eat with a spoon, and much more? Do we not teach them, for example, to greet strangers properly and to behave respectfully? This is precisely what it is like in the training and schooling of a weanling, which is basically now old enough to go to kindergarten and can gain a wealth of knowledge before the real work begins.

If the trainer has laid the foundations for a good education in the suckling phase, the task will not be very difficult. At the same time, be prepared for changes of behaviour in the young horse. These are perfectly normal. Don't be surprised if exercises and lessons which the suckling performed beautifully, suddenly cease to work. Remember that the foal is going through a process of development, which is taking place comparatively quickly. This will be very obvious in the rate of growth of the horse. This development not only affects the body but also the mental state of the horse. The most important aspect influencing this phase of development and learning is the required independence of the horse, because the mare is no longer present to provide security. You will soon notice that this can become a problem. It may give the trainer the feeling of having to start again from the beginning, and this discourages many people. Nevertheless, the preparatory work with the suckling foal is of inestimable value. If the weanling has not learnt these lessons, the difficulties will be far greater as the insecurity of being alone is linked to basic ignorance: by no means a healthy basis for learning! The trainer will have to expect resistance, which in view of the fact that the foal has by now gained considerable strength and agility, will almost certainly cause problems. It could well lead to the trust that was built up between horse and human being lost, and trust can never be regained as easily as it was gained during the suckling phase of the foal.

PRE-REQUISITES AND PROBLEMS

Keeping the weanling in a horse-friendly environment is, of course, the pre-requisite for training a physically and mentally fit horse. Neither should correct feeding, medical care (worming, inoculations) or regular hoof-care be neglected. They form the basis for the foal's

A horse-friendly schooling and environment is the pre-requisite for raising a physically and mentally fit horse.

health and also for successful schooling and training. Naturally, the correct environment also includes the companionship of other foals of the same age as well as older horses. When the weanling returns to its home stable after a sufficiently long period of separation, it must be re-integrated into its old herd. If there are no companions of the same age available, a difficult time will begin for the young horse. Although weaned from the mother, yearlings are still children. Like children, they continue to learn from older horses and have the need to play, test their strength, and frolic about. The need for companions of the same age group, will continue for some time. Never forget that horses are not really mature until the age of six or seven.

If you have decided to buy a weanling or a yearling, the conditions of its schooling at its breeder's must be examined. Was the suckling foal able to live with others of a similar age? Did it have sufficient space? Did it receive the appropriate inoculations and worming doses? Were the hooves checked frequently? What was the feeding like? These and many other questions are decisive for the horse's future, as many things omitted during the suckling period can never be regained!

If you purchase a badly raised foal which was neither cared for sufficiently nor taught the basics of training, you will not have an easy time of it with your weanling. If the foal is already suffering health problems, this will cause untold difficulties. As a rule, a horse will by accompanied by the sins of its early childhood for its entire life.

A horse will suffer for life from the consequences of a bad schooling.

The schooling aim for a yearling is primarily to establish the relationship between man and horse. In this context, it is not so much what is being done as doing something with it at all.

If schooling is neglected in the first six months when the foal is with its mother, the trainer will have much catching up to do. It will be difficult, although not impossible, to school and train to a satisfactory level a horse which is more or less undomesticated. In any case, this is not a task for an uncertain and fearful human, but instead requires specific experience. Mistakes made during the training of a young horse always emerge sooner or later, but an experienced trainer will be capable of getting even a two- or three-year-old into shape. If you want to enjoy greater pleasure with your horse, however, it is better to deal with the right things at the appropriate stage. The childhood and youth of the horse, between the age of six months to two years, should not be wasted.

If it has been taught adequately in its first six months the demands placed on the yearling will not be excessive although lessons for the youngster may have to be repeated over and over, in order to consolidate them and try them out in new situations (in the absence of the dam). At the age of one, it is not very important what you do with the youngster as long as he is being taught something. The primary aim of the schooling period in the first and second year is to strengthen the relationship with and trust of the young horse. Much

needs to be done to achieve this goal. The weanling will have learned many things and these now serve to strengthen the bond and mutual trust between horse and trainer. Once you are aware of how important the horse's trust and your life long relationship with it is, you will realise how useful the period after weaning actually is.

Be aware, however, of becoming over-enthusiastic. In principle, it is a good thing to do a lot of things with young horses. All tasks that are mentally demanding for the horse should

Picking up the yearling's feet should by now have become part of its routine.

ster intensively for 10 to 15 minutes. A further 15 minutes can then be spent on exercises which are already part of the routine, and then don't forget to spend some time stroking, scratching and just talking – simply being together!

REFRESHING THE LESSONS LEARNED SO FAR

It is of great advantage if you can spend at least as much time with a yearling as you would with a horse that has been broken. The time you would spend with the older horse on its back, can be spent refreshing the lessons learned so far, extending them, and also simply being with the foal. This type of approach promotes the relationship and trust automatically and, in future, new tasks will benefit from this. The less demanding the tasks are, the longer can be devoted to them.

Picking up and picking out the yearling's feet should by now have become a daily routine. Certainly, the farrier will already have seen the foal's hooves a few times. If work had to be done on the hoof on these occasions – whether to correct a malformation or to cut back the hoof and frog – the young horse will also have learned to stand on three legs for a more prolonged time. In the case of very young foals, necessary treatment from the farrier should be split into several phases with frequent rests in between, the reason being that the foals soon become impatient and tire

be practised for no more than 15 minutes at a time. The young horse is unable to concentrate for a longer period. If it is pushed too hard, the exercise will no longer be executed successfully and the horse will become fidgety. This means ending the session with bad results, which is counterproductive for the overall training. Less is more therefore. However that does not mean spending no more than 15 minutes with the horse in all. As a rule, you can work a young-

very quickly. Now, the period during which the hoof is picked up can be lengthened with a yearling. If you feel able to treat your own horse's hooves you will have to use the rasp more frequently and round off the hoof edge, in order to avoid the hooves breaking up. This is the best chance to match the tasks you undertake to the capabilities of the foal. It is preferable to work in more frequent and short stages than for one long continual stretch. In this context, it should however be pointed out that in the United Kingdom any farriery work may only be carried out by a qualified farrier. For the sake of your horse's health and well-being, frequent visits by the farrier (every six to eight weeks) should be a matter of course.

Other activities which can be carried out regularly are rubbing oil into the coronet band and rinsing the hooves with water. Of course, we would advise not to exaggerate the rubbing-in of oil or the oiling of the yearling's hooves; the main point is to accustom the horse to the necessary care procedures. To start getting the youngster used to this, it is sufficient to pass a dry (or wet) brush over the coronet band. Once hoof-care has become routine it needs to be practised regularly for the rest of the horse's life and never be given up. If problems occur, the process needs to be repeated more frequently ("trial runs", so to speak). For horses who do not present any problems, on the other hand, the regular and necessary hoof-care also acts as training.

Finally, the horse can already be prepared for its first shoeing by knocking gently on the hoof edge with a rubber mallet or similar tool to simulate the hammering-in of horseshoe nails. If any malformations have to be corrected or if hoof problems (illnesses) occur, some horses may need to be fitted with shoes even as yearlings. In this case, you can give yourself a pat on the back if you carried out the early acclimatisation training. There is nothing worse than a foal rushing about in fear and uncertainty whilst being shod, a trait which will usually continue into later life due to this initial bad experience.

Putting on a headcollar every day helps the horse become used to routine handling.

Depending on the conditions of the stable management, both fitting a headcollar and leading the young horse will already be part of the daily routine.

If the young horses spend day and night out in the field and are not stabled at all, the daily task of putting on a headcollar may be deemed unnecessary. In spite of this, it should be done simply for the purpose of training. Why not take a little walk around the field, which will only take ten minutes? This will be all it needs to remind the yearling of the headcollar-breaking and leading lessons.

It is also quite useful to take the foal into the stable from the field in order to groom it and practise picking up its feet. In any case, part of the daily routine of the responsible horse owner should be examination of the horse for injuries, so the two can be combined. Also find some time to stroke the foal extensively, something it will enjoy greatly. The young horse can also be given its mineral and hard feed rations on this occasion. On no account, however, should you feed the yearling titbits with your hand. If, for instance, the yearling is given titbits to make catching

Loading – without the support of the mother – can lead to slight uncertainty. Therefore this lesson should also be taught frequently.

it in the field easier, it will refuse to come to you if your pockets are empty. Quite apart from that, horses learn very quickly where the titbits are and begin searching around the jacket pockets for them and then grabbing and snapping at them. Not only is this particularly annoying, but it can also become quite dangerous. This is a quick way of raising a "biter." Both the daily hard feed and the occasional titbit, given as a reward, should be placed in the designated feed trough or in a bowl placed on the floor.

Even in the later schooling stages of the riding horse, during ground training or work under the saddle, you should refrain from rewarding the horse by feeding it titbits. As a rule, this is usually more a question of bribery than of a reward. You should only use feed as an enticement or reward in exceptional circumstances and for certain lessons (to make it clear to the horse what it should do), and even then only for a short time. Appropriate reference is given in this book where such exceptional cases occur. In all other situations, using feed as an integrated part of the schooling process will have a negative rather than a positive effect.

Feeding titbits with the hand as a reward can have unpleasant consequences and should, therefore, only be done in exceptional circumstances.

FREQUENTLY EXECUTED TASKS

Make sure that your youngster has plenty of variety in addition to the routine tasks of daily handling. New ideas broaden the abilities of the horse as well as its mental horizons. Variety ensures that the activity will always remain interesting and will never bore the horse.

In principle, you can work on the basis that all tasks which are not physically demanding or cause strain to weanlings and yearlings are suitable exercises. Lungeing, for example, and any kind of strain on the horse's back are of course taboo. This rule applies strictly to all horses – whether they mature early or late. Yearlings are not capable of bearing this type of strain over a prolonged period. Any strain the horse suffers as a youngster will wreak its revenge in old age. The saying that working the horse one year too early will cost it five years of its life is only too true.

There are, however, plenty of exercises for the schooling of yearlings which can be incorporated into the training schedule. How does your youngster react to being hosed down with water? Or when walking through a puddle? Many horses are sceptical about water. Even if the suckling courageously jumped into the stream after its mother, this by no means implies that the weanling will now go through a stream or puddle voluntarily. To begin with, the young horse should be familiarised with the hose pipe. For this purpose, the foal is led over the hose and finally the hose is moved on the

Many horses are suspicious of the water element. Becoming accustomed to hose and water is therefore an excellent training exercise for yearlings.

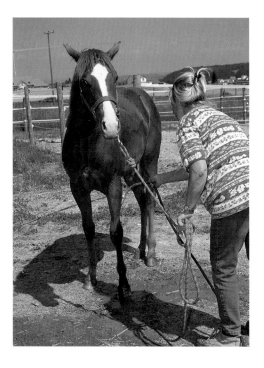

ground, until the animal no longer shows any fear. Only then is the tap turned on and water allowed to flow at low pressure. Allow the horse to smell the hose and water before carefully spraying its hooves.

Some horses will allow you to do this without resistance, others try to jump away or raise the leg with a jerk. If the horse feels insecure, take a wet sponge instead and wipe it down its legs, squeezing the water out in the process. Youngsters are more likely to accept this. Once the yearling has wet legs, it will accept the water from the hose more readily. The horse is slowly accustomed to the wet, preferably by wiping down the legs with a sponge and then with the familiar trainer's hands with water flowing over them An assistant should hold the foal by the headcollar rather than tying up the youngster. Tying up increases the risk of injuries and trauma, for example, if the horse takes fright and, panic-stricken, pulls back and tugs at the rope with all its might. A horse that associates terrible experiences with being tied up, may be difficult to secure in future.

Only after the young horse calmly accepts being sprayed on its legs with the hose should you start moving over the remainder of the body. (Warning: always omit the head!)

Another exercise which must be practised for a long time, depending on the speed of the horse's acceptance, is the use of a spray-bottle. In an emergency, if a horse injures itself and you have to spray the injury with disinfectant, you will appreciate the usefulness of this lesson. Not only that, but fly repellent can be spread more easily over the horse's coat with a spray bottle. These repellents are therefore usually sold in a bottle with a spray top and are quite practical to use. To practise this, take an empty bottle, fill it with water, and slowly begin spraying the neck and chest, until the horse no longer responds nervously. You should be aware that the horse is not primarily afraid of the liquid itself, but rather of the hissing noise it makes. By repeating this exercise often, the horse will soon become familiar with the sound.

At this stage you should also start the desensitisation process with regard to sounds and objects. This is the beginning of the so-called sacking-out training, which every horse should go through in order to lose its fear of everyday objects of our modern life. Thus, you can specifically accustom the young horse to the noise of passing tractors, lorries and motorbikes. If the foal was taken on excursions at its mother's side when it was younger, it will already be used to traffic. In this case, intensifying this acclimatisation training should not present a big problem. Observing all safety measures (never wrap the rope around the hand, provide enough room to move out of the way, stay in a fenced-off area, ensure there are no other distractions), the youngster is led past a tractor with its engine running. Later on, the driver of the tractor can be instructed to drive past the horse.

A start should also be made on getting the yearling used to sweat rugs and numnahs. For this purpose, first take a small blanket and let the foal sniff it. Once it loses interest in the

Trite as it may sound, spraying fly repellent from a spray bottle must be practised, as many young horses are afraid of the hissing noise made by the bottle.

blanket touch the youngster on the shoulder with it, pass it over its neck and finally over its entire body. Make sure not to forget the legs and back. If the horse remains calm, a larger blanket is used and the procedure repeated. If the horse permits this without resistance and nervousness, the whole blanket can be placed over its back. This is the first step towards being saddled or backed later on.

If the lesson with the blanket is a success, the desensitisation training is extended by using a plastic bag and at a later stage a larger plastic tarpaulin. The acclimatisation process

The desensitisation training can be expanded with plastic tarpaulins.

uncertainty, which, however, does not lead to it running away. If you do too much, the horse will lose its trust in its trainer and many hours of schooling will have been for nothing. It is better to proceed slowly and thoughtfully rather than risking a step back. Experience shows that things progress much more quickly, the more time you invest.

REMAINING ALONE

Horses are gregarious animals; therefore you will repeatedly encounter the problem that your youngster does not enjoy remaining alone. It is precisely for this reason that it is important to practise this particular exercise very often. The weanling clings more strongly to its companions in the herd because it seeks to compensate for the loss of its mother. To be separated from the herd in the wild means grave danger for the horse and for a foal it spells almost certain death. Like the flight instinct, the herding instinct is in-built by nature, as a protection to ensure the survival of the species. It is particularly difficult to weaken it and it can never be completely rooted out either through schooling or breeding measures. Therefore, both man and beast must learn to cope with it.

Regular repetition will lead to the youngster becoming used to being on it own, the best way for it to learn to stay alone. An escape-proof paddock or a completely closed

is started from the beginning with each new object. The horse needs to have the opportunity to initially inspect the supposedly dangerous thing by smelling it. Of course, the entire procedure is carried out with care and the horse must never be expected to do more than it is capable of. Don't let the horse panic and try to escape. At the most it may show a slight

loose box is required to ensure that the young horse can be left alone safely. If it was prepared for weaning as a suckling, by learning to be alone for a shorter and then longer period of time, the yearling soon realises that the separation from its companions will not last for ever. If the young horse is neighing its heart out, someone should be left in the stable to supervise it. In most cases a human can offer little support even if there is a good relationship with the horse – because the yearling will only be satisfied with other horses. Speaking to it calmly will do little to help, but can do no harm either. As a comfort some tasty hard feed might be offered, which helps many horses cope with being alone. If the horse is very nervous you should not feed it as the foal in its excitement might swallow the wrong way or may eat too hastily. That could mean risking a blockage in the throat or colic.

After much repetition the yearling will accept the situation and will react in a more relaxed manner to being separated. Make sure not to exaggerate the length of the period of separation otherwise you will achieve the opposite and the horse will cling all the more. The better the young animal copes with being alone, the longer it can be separated from its companions.

Those horses which have been handled more often, usually cope better with being alone. The so-called "wild" youngsters find it more difficult. Therefore, it is worthwhile supporting the horse according to its abilities and spending a lot of time with it (which does not

always necessarily mean work and schooling), so that it will be able to cope with the modern world which rarely matches its natural instincts.

EXCURSIONS ON THE LEAD REIN

You should keep up the excursions outside the yard which the young foal undertook with its dam. For this purpose, it is necessary that the foal has learned to lead well. If this is not the case, leading lessons need to be practised in a fenced-in area.

It is quite possible that the weanling will refuse violently to take a single step out of the yard without its mother or another horse. In this case, it doesn't help pulling on the lead-rope either. If the foal plants its hooves firmly into the ground and refuses to take a single step forward you must not give in to the youngster. This would be an ideal "opportunity" to raise a "clinging horse" of some calibre. Later on, you will be unable to hack out the horse on its own if it does not learn to undertake independent excursions in the company of a human.

Since you should use as little force as possible I do not recommend using the whip to drive the horse forward in this case. The foal would simply move forward out of fear of the whip (which unfortunately is used all too often as an instrument of punishment) – if at all. Certainly, at this stage a light touch would

On excursions, it is advisable for the sake of safety to attach a lead rein with chain to the headcollar, thus having better control over the young horse.

as much patience as older animals, you can also simply stand in one position and wait until the youngster runs out of patience. If you leave to the young horse the decision whether to stand in one place or walk, most decide to walk. The only direction you must firmly prevent the youngster from going is backward.

More is achieved with the young horse through patience and consistency than through punishment.

very rarely be enough. There is a temptation to use the whip in such a way as to cause the horse pain. This should be avoided.

You will often be more successful if you push the youngster forward with your hand on its thigh. An assistant will be of great help here if the foal is already very big. It is a useful trick to lead the foal in zigzag lines. If its neck is bent to the left or right, it cannot resist in the same way as if its head was straight. Most young horses will take their first step this way. Even if they stop again after two steps, the whole action can be repeated. Soon this becomes too uncomfortable for the youngster and it then decides to walk along. As young horses do not possess

If this hurdle has been overcome, the excursions should not last too long while the youngster is uncertain outside the yard. After all, it has never been out alone in the past. For increased safety, it is recommended to attach a second lead rein with chain to the horse, giving you more control over the animal in an emergency. However, careful handling of this lead-rope is essential to avoid causing the youngster unnecessary pain via the chain.

You can only guarantee the safety of the person leading the horse, and the horse itself, by working with care. This includes the choice of appropriate routes. Horses, which are still uncertain must not be led along very busy roads, but instead on quiet woodland paths and field tracks in close proximity to the stable. The lead rein with chain is also part of the

When the foal was allowed to run free alongside its dam, it was permitted to pick to its hearts content along the way; the yearling should no longer be allowed to do this.

safety equipment, and it cannot be repeated often enough that the lead-rope must never be wrapped around your hand. If the foal gets a fright and jumps away, the rope will be pulled tight around the hand and you may be unable to let go. Although the foal is not as powerful as a mature horse, it is quite capable of dragging the person leading it, with the risk of considerable injury. This type of accident has

on occasion led to fatalities. Despite the fun you try to have in handling the horse, safety must never be forgotten. This particularly applies to youngsters, as they do not feel as secure as older, experienced horses.

As a foal, the young horse was allowed to run free beside its mother, as long as the surroundings permitted it. This meant that it was able to pick at grass and smell flowers along the way. Naturally, it will also try to do this when led by its trainer. With a view to its use as a riding horse at a later stage, this picking on the way should no longer be permitted. It is a bad habit, difficult to break in a riding horse if it was allowed to graze like this when young. It can be very awkward for the rider if the horse keeps picking at grass during a ride or walk, quite apart from the danger of snatching at and ingesting a poisonous plant by mistake.

As soon as you put a headcollar or bridle on the horse, this means "work". All my horses learn that feeding is "out" when on the lead-rope or in a bridle. It is much more pleasant to work with horses trained this way. I can leave a saddled or bridled horse in a field, perhaps even beside a grazing horse, without the concern that it will drop its head and begin eating. If it did this, it could step on the reins, and would almost certainly run away and try to escape my control. When a horse eats it pays no attention to the trainer's instructions.

Therefore, picking at the wayside must not be permitted. Horses are allowed to graze as much and as long as they like in the field. Here is where they have their leisure time, not whilst on the lead-rope or later under the saddle. Standing firm on this issue is by no means heartless but serves to ensure safety and discipline. It also simplifies handling the animal. The horse will no longer constantly pull on the lead-rope to get to a blade of grass, but instead will be gentle and easy to lead. This makes not only the horse owner, but also the horse, feel better.

LEADING THE YOUNGSTER FROM ANOTHER MOUNT

Yearlings trained in a horse-friendly manner abound with energy and enterprise. Depending on the breed and temperament they can also prove to be very temperamental on the lead-rope and will use every opportunity to measure their strength. If the young horse becomes too over-confident this can lead to problems whilst out on walks.

It is often better to control a young animal from the saddle of another horse if the ridden mount is absolutely safe and calm and displays no animosity towards the young horse and if the yearling can be tied to the saddle without being able to break free. A young horse will calm down very quickly next to an older lead horse if its wild manners are due to nervousness and fear. However, if the foal is simply jumping about because it is full of itself and overflowing with temperament, the odds are stacked against you at your the end of the lead-rope (even with a stallion chain). If you tie the lead-rope to the saddle horn (western saddle) or girth, the youngster can pull and jump about as much as it wants, but cannot break free. So it learns very quickly that rebelling is pointless. Of course, an absolutely quiet and reliable lead mount is essential. (Beware! The small D-rings on the English saddle do not withstand the strain of the lead-rope. The girth is a much better attaching point.)

Under no circumstances should the lead-rope be tied to the saddle during trotting or cantering. If the young horse stumbles, the pull of the rope could cause it to fall and injure itself. Therefore, tying the lead-rope is only recommended when you walk. At any pace faster than a walk the lead-rope must be held in the hand. And never forget the first rule when leading a horse: "Never wrap the rope around the hand!"

When leading the weanling from another mount, for safety reasons the lead-rope should only be fastened to the saddle during the walk.

Another advantage of leading the youngster from another horse is that it can be exercised during these outings at the trot and canter, something you cannot do on foot. The outings can be extended thus improving the condition of the young horse.

In the case of weanlings which have been re-integrated into the "old" herd, the dam can be used as the riding horse. At this stage, of course, it no longer possible to let the foal run along without a lead-rope, for it has become independent and could wander off on its own. It has to remain on the lead-rope and by so doing learns to walk along in a disciplined way and follow the instructions of the rider.

In addition, just as does the dam or other mount used, the foal hears the voice commands which the rider uses, for example, for a transition of paces. Thus the yearling learns these automatically through frequent repetition. This prepares the horse for its advanced schooling.

TETHERING AND STANDING STILL

Our yearling is now running along quite well on the lead from another horse and also leads on foot without any resistance.It is now ready to learn other lessons. Being led from another horse, the foal learned to accept being tied to the ridden horse. Basically, the young horse also remembers this from its days as a suckling when it learned to be led tied to the mare's surcingle. This means in general that it is ready to be tethered. Naturally, this will initially be done next to another horse and under constant supervision. The lead-rope should be tied with a quick-release knot to a beam or tethering ring intended for this purpose. This means that it can be undone quickly in an emergency.

It is very useful to tether the horse during its daily care, because the horse is standing directly next to you so you can watch it and respond quickly if there are any problems. The horse should now accept without any difficulty that it can neither run away nor that the lead-rope will give. Thus it will not try to resist being tethered by pulling away with all its strength. It has learned that it cannot break free anyway, and so it accepts the given situa-

Now is time for the yearling to learn to be tethered and stand still.

tion. Do, however, observe the following: never frighten the horse on purpose and thereby activate its escape reflex (for example, through sacking out training carried out incorrectly). Also, do not tie it up for too long and, initially, never alone as this could frighten it. In the beginning, it is enough to tether the horse for as long as it is being groomed. Slowly the period of tethering is extended and the horse is made to wait for five minutes after grooming has finished, and then it is let back into the paddock. Finally, the young horse is brought in from the field, simply to tie it up for ten minutes. It is then released back into the field. During this period of tethering it is also useful to give the yearling its hard feed ration or to offer it some hay if it seems impatient or nervous. Later on – i.e. after a few years – the horse will be tied for longer periods as a matter of course. Whether it is resting while out on a long hack or is tied up during shoeing, the question of being tethered will no longer be an issue. I condemn tying up yearlings in a riding school yard for hours (possibly even in the midday sun with no shade) in order to teach them patience, something I observe happening time and time again. These methods must and should not be used as horses learn patience automatically with increasing age and correct handling. It is sheer torture to expect a yearling to stand on one spot for hours on end. This method compares to the breaking-in – in the literal sense – of horses!

No one expects a three-year-old-child to sit quietly at a table for hours. Adults, on the other hand, do this voluntarily during conferences, at work or during their leisure time in the pub. In the same way a young horse is still impatient and thirsty for action, so expecting it to be tethered for several hours is pure torture. For a grown horse, on the other hand, this presents no problem if the animal is slowly introduced to being tied up and, as it gets older, the length of time is also increased with care.

With increasing patience (which of course improves with every training session) the horse also learns about standing still. For this purpose, the horse does not necessarily have to be tied up. Whether it is being saddled and mounted later in life or during the daily horse care session (grooming, picking out feet) – standing still not only means a larger measure of safety for the horse owner, but also makes handling the horse much easier. It is not exactly pleasant, if a restless horse tramples on your toes!

It is not an easy task to teach a young horse calmly to keep standing still. You should be satisfied with a few seconds which can gradually be extended to minutes. If the rider demands it a disciplined, mature mount will stand for even half an hour without being tied up. But it is a long journey to get to that point: a journey which should be started when the horse is still a foal.

It is only wise to begin the exercise if the surroundings are suitable. Calm should prevail in the stable or yard and, if the exercise is to succeed, nothing should distract the horse. The horse is expected to stand still calmly on hearing the appropriate command (for example "Whoa" or "Stand") and a gentle tug on the lead-rope. This is always done, for example, before the horse is tied up or you have to perform a task on the horse. Now, each step the horse moves away must be corrected firmly. This is the most important part of the whole training exercise to teach the horse to stand. Therefore the horse should be led (without being either punished or praised) immediately back to the designated spot and the voice command repeated clearly. Each movement should to be nipped in the bud, if possible. If the horse lifts its hoof from the ground, correction must follow immediately.

If the horse stands still, the level of safety for the handler is greatly increased for all tasks performed.

longer. However, your efforts will only be crowned with success if you carry out the work with consistency and don't let the youngster get away with taking a single step. Soon the young animal will accept that it has no chance to break away as the trainer corrects any attempt immediately. A yearling is only expected to stand still for a few seconds; then it is praised and led away, to make it clear to it that the exercise is over. It is especially important that the exercise is always terminated before the horse becomes impatient and begins to fidget. This requires a certain amount of intuitive power and expertise. If you demand that the youngster stand still for too long a period it will become unsettled and the exercise cannot be finished off satisfactorily.

You must never expect the horse to stand still without being tethered if the training area is not fenced off. In addition, the young horse should not be left without supervision because intelligent horses learn very quickly that once the trainer is out of sight they are no longer within their sphere of control!

You will require a large amount of patience, but even more importantly, persistence, if the young horse is to learn to stand still.

Some horses grasp very quickly that they must not move from the spot, others take

GAMES AND TRICKS?

If the exercises and lessons described are still insufficient to occupy the horse's potential for activities, or if the trainer would like to introduce more variety into the foal's training schedule, other types of exercise are available.

However these should be chosen carefully in order not to overtax the horse physically or mentally. After all, everything you do can be exaggerated. The temptation to give in to the half-grown horse's play instinct and to mime the role of its companions in the field can arise very quickly. Foals are amenable to every type of chasing game and after all want to test their strength in playful fights. This can soon lead to biting and kicking (with no ill-will intended). This is where the fun stops! A foal's hooves could seriously injure a human. If a foal is permitted to kick humans as a youngster it will continue to do so later on. The result will be a horse which bites and kicks and which eventually will become so dangerous that handling it can be life threatening.

Therefore, the category of forbidden games, even at this early stage, includes rearing, snapping, and kicking anywhere in the vicinity of humans. There is no great merit in teaching a horse to rear; this no longer impresses anyone. Any expert trainer will condemn this type of trick. At best these exercises belong in the circus ring and this is where they should remain.

Nevertheless, there are lessons the horse can be taught without any danger. These assist the horse's mental, as well as physical flexibility. In addition, the animal attains a better co-ordination.

Let your imagination run free when choosing exercises, making sure that the horse is never overtaxed at this tender age. You should wait until young horses are at least two years old before teaching advanced equitation movements such as lying down, Spanish Walk, and

Complement (see p.119 ff.). The preparatory work for this, however, can begin at this stage and the leading lessons, which are described in greater depth on p. 117 ff., can be intensified. If the horse is very obedient at this stage, exercises such as lifting the legs can be attempted.

FOALS GROWN UP WILD AND PROBLEM CASES

If you are given a weanling which reacts quite wildly, does not lead, even rears on the lead-rope, or bucks occasionally, you will have to catch up on a lot of groundwork. The suckling was most probably not prepared sufficiently, or the owner was too "smitten" with the charm of his or her foal and did not discipline the young horse enough. Certainly there are very temperamental as well as calmer youngsters, but it is essential for the owner to have control over the horse in every situation in order to eliminate any danger to man or beast.

An untamed foal must learn discipline and obedience urgently, even if this sometimes requires drastic measures. Children, too, require some disciplining now and again to turn them into decent human beings. Therefore, you should never allow any disobedience because everything the horse is allowed to do as a foal it will also think permissible when it is older. Always keep this in mind when handling a young animal.

Thus, if the youngster playfully bites or sucks and chews the trainer's fingers (often a need for the suckling), it must be stopped. Once the horse is two years old, these playful actions are not quite so pleasant any more. As a rule, a gentle tap is enough to keep the foal in line. They realise quite quickly what they may and may not do.

At the age of one year, it is high time to take care of the serious schooling of the foal. Once the horse is two years old, it will be very difficult to keep it within its limits due to its strength, size and sexual maturity. In such a case it sometimes requires brute force to tame the animal. Things should never be allowed to get to that point.

The schooling and training of a foal is always the task of an experienced horseman/woman. If you still feel uncertain about handling foals you should seek help early on. It is better to seek advice before the horse is out of control because any correction of acquired vices will be twice as hard and take much longer than a sound and expert schooling.

A foal should never be entrusted to a child. The sight of the young child and darling little foal may seem sweet but can so easily spell disaster. The initially well-intentioned idea of letting the foal and toddler "grow up together" is ultimately doomed to failure. The foal will treat the child in the same way it would other members of its species. Any human can imagine what this means. In addition, a child, which itself still needs lessons in upbringing, will never be able to impart the necessary schooling to another individual. Rearing a foal is, therefore, a task for adults who must also have the

necessary experience in handling horses in general.

The less schooling and training the young horse has had, the more severe will be the measures needed to discipline the yearling or an older horse. Since no horse lover wants this, consistent handling should be implemented from the start. This in no way excludes fairness towards the horse. On the contrary, it means finding the correct balance of punishment, correction and praise, which need to be meted out as an immediate response in order to be successful. With good trainers, the balance of praise and punishment will lie at around 90 per cent praise and 10 per cent punishment. The character of the horse, however, will also play its part in this ratio.

In the case of difficult horses – whether they have been incorrectly handled (which is more often the case) or they have a bad character – more time is needed for training and schooling. This additional effort will certainly be worthwhile because you will profit from it later on. Other problems will present themselves at the backing stage and a good preparation will make life easier.

A frequent mistake is that problems that occur during schooling are often ignored and the assumption is made that they will solve themselves as the horse matures. This will certainly not happen; in fact the problem will become more pronounced. Therefore, you should never put off anything for too long. The sooner you discipline your horse, the better.

FIRST PUBLIC APPEARANCES

Attending championship shows for foals and show classes for breeding stock is an absolute must for the professional breeder to present his young-stock. At these events the young-stock will be assessed and compared with the foals of other breeders. Judging is particularly important for the breeder, because the results will influence the foal's selling price and give him an indication of whether the pairing of dam and stallion has fulfilled the breeder's expectations.

But even if you only breed as a hobby you cannot avoid presenting your foal if the young horse is to be registered with its respective breed association and receive its breeding documents. (Hot iron branding is not practised in Great Britain but is an essential process for young horses in some countries.) The breeding documents (and brand numbers in certain countries) are important for the identification of the foal. If the breeding and the exact age can be proven by documentary evidence the market value of the horse is higher than that of a horse whose origin is uncertain. Even the breeder who only breeds as a hobby and has no

For the professional breeder, the presentation of his young-stock at championship classes for foals is particularly important.

intention of selling his foal should have his foal freeze marked and register it with the breed association to get the horse's papers, if only to protect against theft.

The leisure rider may want to present his foal at shows and events, either to accustom the horse to such situations or simply to exhibit his youngster. When the foal is still accompanied by its dam, such outings usually turn out very well as the mare spells security for the young horse and helps to soothe its nerves. However attending various events with a yearling is a challenge as the horse is now on its own and has to place absolute trust in its owner.

PREPARATION FOR
HORSE SHOWS

Perhaps the mare and foal have been transported to freeze marking appointments or horse shows in the past. But the situation is quite different when journeys are undertaken with the young horse on its own. In this case, it proves very useful if loading and travelling have already become routine. Now the foal simply has to be turned out smartly to display it to its best advantage. By now, the youngster should also lead safely on the lead-rope and stand still. Young horses which show unruly behaviour and fight against the person leading them during the presentation leave nothing but a negative impression. The judges cannot assess them properly. Therefore walking and trotting in hand should be practised in a designated school

at home. Even standing the horse correctly must be practised, and you should find out in advance how the animals have to stand. In in-hand classes for western horse breeds the foals are required to stand in a closed position. Warm bloods, on the other hand, should be presented "open" so that the judges are able to see all four legs from the side on.

Always bear in mind that very highly bred horses can become nervous at a show and can even jump about despite the best preparation at home. If matters don't work out so well the first time round there is always a second chance.

Quite apart from this, you must never overestimate the results of breeding stock classes. What use is the most perfect conformation if the character of the horse leaves much to be desired? In a show class the horse presented can only be judged with regard to conformation because only the owner knows his foal inside out and knows its value to him/her. Don't, therefore, be discouraged by bad results. I know a mare which was placed second from the bottom in a broodmare class. The judges thought that the horse was not typical of its breed and lacked in good conformation. This mare, however, developed into one of the best performance horses in Germany. It was able to compensate its weaknesses in build with an incomparable will and willingness to perform.

At the same time, you always want to present your youngster in the best possible light. This involves the correct care of the foal. The hooves must be kept clean and the coat well groomed. Depending on the breed, the mane should be plaited (warm-bloods, hunters, etc.).

Show classes for young-stock should not be overestimated It is almost impossible to assess the character of the horse which, however, is at least as important as a good conformation.

The tail hangs better if it is plaited on the day before the show and is undone and well brushed shortly before the class. The hair will be wavy and create a fuller effect. However, if the tail is very short it is better to leave it alone.

For all these preparations the foal must be fairly easy to handle by now because it needs to let you work on its hooves, groom and wash it. Leading and loading are important pre-requisites to be able to present a foal successfully at a show.

The horse's correct stance must be practised at home so that it goes well at the show. Good preparation may contribute to a good placing and maybe even to a victory.

TAKING FOALS TO HORSE SHOWS

Taking a weanling to horse shows entails a relatively large amount of effort. If you are travelling with only one horse, you can put the yearling into the other stall. In this case it is necessary, however, to have at least one "extra" assistant present who will spend his time exclusively looking after the young horse. It will be his/her task to show the yearling the show ground, the collecting ring and the spectators. This has to be done in such a way as not to hinder any of the participating horses and riders.

Often the weanling will cling to the show horse (which usually is a stablemate in any case), and this can lead to problems separating them at the show ground. In this case, the participation or possible success of the experienced horse in its classes is in question. You need to take this into account beforehand. It is therefore sometimes better to transport the young horse alone and not to enter any horse at the horse show.

This requires an additional expenditure of energy and is therefore not often done. You will have to decide according to circumstances which method is best. Perhaps there is a horse show in the immediate vicinity which will minimise the expenditure of transport, time and money.

If possible, you should frequently take the opportunity to familiarise the young horse with horse shows and events. Basically, the type of event is not important because there will usually be many people, loud music and unknown horses present.

PROCESSIONS AND CHARITY RIDES

Processions and charity rides are also good opportunities to use. These are being organised with increasing frequency, whether it is processions, charity rides, or other festivities. Here it is appropriate to bring the young horse along on the lead from another mount because it can

be kept under better control this way. An additional assistant, who leads the foal on the off side, may also provide additional support.

Sometimes it is quite enough to lead the young horse around the assembly area a few times and then take it back home in order not to expose it to the bustle for too long. The type and length of activity the horse can attend always depends on the horse's nerves. Nothing should be forced and the safety of horse and man must be a main concern. Ideally, the noise level and numbers of people should gradually increase with time. Unfortunately you have no control over this, even when the type of event is known. If it is done every year in similar fashion, you will know roughly what to expect.

Certainly, it is sensible to bring along nervous horses only in the company of a stablemate. But the aim must be to encourage the young animal's independence as soon as possible as you will otherwise have a lifelong fight with a nappy horse.

THE TWO-YEAR-OLD HORSE

REACHING SEXUAL MATURITY

Another year has passed and the young horse has become bigger and more mature. Some two-year-old horses still look like a foal, others give the impression of a fully grown horse. This depends on the breed, but also on the upbringing, the keeping and feeding conditions. Usually the animals are still growing in all directions and it would be wrong to speak of a beautiful horse. The leap from yearling to

Stallions are not always easy to control due to their sexual drive. Only consistent schooling and an expert hand are a guarantee of handling an entire without risk.

two-year-old however can be so enormous for some horses that you may start thinking of backing it, and many horse owners in fact do this. Horse breeding has produced so-called early- and late-maturing horses, which enables the use of one breed earlier on and another not until later. Despite this, I would like to state emphatically in advance that, in my opinion, a two-year-old is too young to ride. Even if the physical pre-requisites are present, the horse will not be psychologically mature. In addition, it is only later that the strain placed on a horse too young to cope with it will show

itself, when signs of wear and tear become apparent. Money is certainly a ruling factor for professional trainers and breeders, where the early use of a horse will mean greater profit.

Private horse owners, however, who amount to almost 95 per cent of all people who keep horses, are able to and should wait until the horse is at least three years old. Even at the age of two years there is a lot the horse owner can do to ensure good training and basic schooling, so that the eventual breaking-in process itself presents no problems.

A major event in the life of a horse is the attainment of sexual maturity, which usually happens at the age of two, but can sometimes occur later or earlier. You will observe a change in behaviour which many horse owners have difficulties in coping with. Stallions especially will engage in power struggles and these of course also with humans. This means that you will have to decide about castration, because a good many owners of young entires find out to their frustration, that handling the stallion is becoming harder and that the owner will soon no longer be able to impose his will.

a flash, if they come near a mare in season. It is generally said that stallions are unpredictable and dangerous. This certainly applies to many entires with a high rank order.

Castration normally means that the animal loses the stallion-like manners, if it has been cut early enough. Geldings are very obliging mounts, and are generally said to have better characteristics than mares, which can also be difficult when they are in season. If the young male horse is to be used exclusively as a riding horse, it is always more sensible to have it gelded.

CASTRATION OF STALLIONS

The character of the young stallion can undergo a serious change on reaching sexual maturity. It can occur as early as the age of twelve or eighteen months. Suddenly the young horse exhibits distinct stallion-like mannerisms, which manifest themselves in kicking and above all in rearing. The young entire stops paying attention to its trainer, concentrating instead entirely on attractive mares. If the previous training has not been consistent, the extent to which the young stallion can be controlled is limited due to its strong sexual urges. There are entires which are obliging and quiet, and whose stallion behaviour is barely noticeable. But as a rule, even their characters can change in

It is generally acknowledged that geldings are the best mounts because the sexual drive, which can cause changes in behaviour that are difficult to handle, has been switched off.

Castration has other important roles. In most riding yards, stallions have to be kept apart. Often they can only be sent out into the field alone or not at all. Putting an entire out with mares who are not meant to be covered by this stallion is impossible. The stallion regards even geldings as rivals and aims to fight them or drive them away. Therefore a stallion will always lead a lonely life, if he is to be used as a riding horse. In addition, he will be in constant conflict with his sex drive, which he may never outlive. Therefore you will do a stallion no favours by not having him cut. As a gelding he can be integrated into a herd and have a much more satisfying life.

If the stallion is to be used for breeding you should consider whether he is at all suitable for this purpose. Only the best horses should be used for breeding, so that only desirable temperament and ability are inherited. These include conformation (which is judged in breeding stock classes) as well as the character of the horse. In addition to the aspects of conformation, the breed-specific type, the temperament, paces and charisma must also be of high quality for the entire to be suited as a stud stallion. A well-mannered stallion always has a good character. If a stallion becomes dangerous and uncontrollable, however, the chances are that he passes on his difficult character. In that case he should be ruled out as a stud stallion.

Professional breeders are prepared for the keep of entires. The essential life-enhancing requirements of the stallion are satisfied by sufficient grazing space and groups of young horses for company. If he is lucky, the stallion will also be allowed out in the field with mares which he is supposed to cover unsupervised. This is the most natural way of keeping an entire and the stallion is happy with it. But these requirements can almost never be offered to a stallion being used as a riding horse.

In most cases therefore young entires are gelded at the age of two. This makes the further schooling and training of the horse considerably easier. If the young horse is to remain a stallion, on the other hand, its upbringing will have to be very consistent, in order to avoid difficulties. The slightest inattention will avenge itself. Therefore raising and training stallions should be left to experienced trainers. Only all too often riders overestimate their abilities to perform this task.

SHOULD TWO-YEAR-OLD MARES BE COVERED?

It is not a rare occurrence that two-year-old mares are covered, which means the foal arrives when the dam is barely three years old. Only then do we concentrate on training the mare to be ridden – if at all. There are three reasons for covering the young mare early. In order to fulfil the requirements of the breed, a certain height in the case of many pony breeds, for example, must not be exceeded. If the mare threatens to grow to be too big, she is covered at the age of two. This method can halt the growth process, because the mare needs more energy for the foal.

Another reason is that the breeder wishes to have a foal as soon as possible, as the sale of young animals means money for him. He does not want the expense and trouble of keeping the mare, which is to be used for

Well-built foals may only be expected from fully grown mares.

breeding purposes, for an extra year, if she can just as well be covered now. Unfortunately it is a phenomenon of our times that horses are utilised at the earliest age possible.

The third reason for covering a two-year-old mare is the attitude that the horse cannot be used as a riding horse at this stage anyway, whereas it could well produce a foal in the meantime. Owners of a two-year-old mare are often not capable of doing anything else with the animal than having it covered. This shows a lack of horse sense, as the age of two is a particularly important time, which should not to be ignored in the schooling and training of the horse. Although many lessons can be done out with a mare in foal, the resulting foal, once it is born, becomes a hindrance for the training of the then three-year-old mare.

But in principle this is not the only reason the two-year-old mare should not be covered. None of the aforementioned reasons is sufficient justification, in my opinion. My view is that covering a two-year-old is simply too early. Why should the young horse not be allowed to enjoy its youth? In addition, carrying a foal exposes a mare's physique to enormous strain. The physical strain is even greater for a mare which is not fully grown, because the early pregnancy will use up substances which she urgently needs for her growth (amongst other things, for the formation of bone material). I would never burden a two-year-old mare with a foal.

As a rule, the foals of two-year old mares are particularly '"weedy", not only because they are first foals, which are often a bit smaller in any case, but because the mare is simply physically overtaxed and cannot therefore produce a big strong foal.

With regard to the objection that mares in the wild are often covered at the age of two, I would argue that most two-year-old mares are covered but do not take. The rate of resorption is relatively high in young mares, which in the wild is primarily due to the availability of food and environmental conditions. If the two-year-old mare were to carry the foal to term, her own life would be in danger due to her poorly developed constitution at that age.

PROBLEMS OF "ADOLESCENCE"

The size and energy of the two-year-old horse has now practically reached its limit. It seems that the youngsters are quite aware of this: they test their strength against other horses, and also against people, if they are permitted. Therefore two-year-olds are often more difficult to handle than weanlings or mature horses. This phase, which can be compared with puberty in teenagers, can continue until the age of four to five years. The behaviour differs from horse to horse, for every horse has its own individual character which has a fairly large influence in this phase. Naturally the behaviour is also dependent on breed. There are horses which are extremely difficult to control at this stage whereas others will always remain as gentle as ever.

RANK ORDER STRUGGLES AMONG THE YOUNG TEENAGERS

Many horse owners are disappointed by their youngster, if they suddenly realise that their well-brought-up and obliging yearling has turned into a rebellious two-year-old, which constantly spoils for a fight. "Did I do something wrong in its education?" you may ask yourself, or, "I always treated him fairly, why has he become so evil?" The change in character can develop to such an extent that you will no longer recognise your own horse. This can even lead to disappointed horse owners deciding to sell their horse. You should however not go to such extremes because every horse owner must realise that this is a case of a phase which will pass. However, you will need to be able to handle it.

Between eighteen months and two years, horses will reach sexual maturity. In the wild this is the time when they have to assert their position within the herd. This is especially true of young entires who are now driven away by the lead stallion, as the youngsters often try at this age to cover the odd mare or so. They will try to steal mares from their own father, which the latter naturally tries to prevent by chasing the young pretenders out of the herd. The young stallions form small bachelor groups and practise their fighting strength, until they are strong enough to take on the lead stallion in a serious fight.

The physical and psychological strength of a young stallion influences the rest of his life. The natural goal of every stallion is reproduction. The drive needs to be very strong so that the survival of the species, including natural selection, is assured. Therefore, the young stallions are particularly aggressive and ready to fight at this stage. You will be able to observe this aggressiveness even within your own herd. The youngsters will continuously provoke the older horses and try to draw them into fights (which are now no longer just playful, but all too often become very serious). It is rare, however, that serious injuries arise from such fights. And the horses also need

these altercations, in order to find emotional balance.

Not only stallions, but also mares now fight amongst themselves more seriously, for the two-year-olds are often covered by the lead stallion, although they seldom take. Primarily the fights concern the hierarchy within the herd. The bigger and stronger the mares become, the sooner they will be able to attain a higher position for themselves. As foals they are always at the bottom of the pecking order. The rank structure can now change. Depending on fitness, temperament and charisma, older animals must

"Young thugs" whose rank in the herd is a high one will also try to assert their power against humans

make way for the next generation. Although age is not the deciding factor in the rank order, but rather type, character and physical constitution, young horses from the age of about two are seriously able to reform the rank structure.

> At the age of two many horses question the rank structure and fight for a better position within the herd.

A successful horse gains a large measure of self-confidence and this can be very useful for its further training. High-ranking horses are often very intelligent and master their tasks easily. The lower-ranked horse hardly changes its character and can therefore often also be handled well by less experienced trainers.

"I MEAN IT!"

High-ranking horses, which have risen within the hierarchy by the age of two, will try one day to assert their position towards humans. And it is precisely at this point that many horse owners become desperate. Suddenly the horse, which has usually been so obedient, rebels against them, goes into attack mode, refuses to move or simply stops obeying any orders. At this stage

some horse lovers are pushed to the limits of their horse sense.

Due to hierarchy struggles, not only stallions, but also mares and entires, which have already been gelded, are not exactly the most obliging animals at the age of two. Handling these young horses therefore requires an expert hand. The horse owner must be doubly watchful, so that he can recognise and deal with the dangers caused by the provocative behaviour of the horse early on.

Due to their awkwardness, many horse owners avoid handling and working with horses at this stage in their lives. But this attitude, which is often simply a protection mechanism (the horse owner really becomes afraid of his horse), can lead to even greater difficulties. If you feel you cannot cope or are in fact afraid of your horse, it is vital to seek the advice and assistance of an expert.

This stage is precisely the time when educational measures are most valuable. If the young horse accepted the human as its superi or as a suckling, this was not the result of educational measures, but because at this age it saw everything and everyone without exception as being stronger. Man contributed nothing to this. Due to its weakness and helplessness the foal needs someone it can trust and who will lead it. But with increasing independence, which begins during weaning, the horse starts to call into question all ranks within the hierarchy. Since the human always has to retain the upper hand over the horse, however, he must not permit any rebelliousness or power struggles. On the contrary, it is of particular importance now to make it clear to the horse through consistent handling, who has the final say. Only at this stage, will it in fact be established who is going to have to obey whom in future. You need to be prepared for this. Even years later many horses will continue to test whether they can up their ranking just that little bit more. Rebellion in one form or another will establish itself at some point. Later, however, the horses will give in more easily, if they have been put in their place early enough.

But now – in their youthful exuberance – they really want to know. If you don't lay down the rules during this phase, you will create a real problem.

If the horses behaviour is unruly, that does not mean that it has become evil. You know on the contrary that it is testing the rank order. Of course it is senseless to engage in a fight with the horse, as you would very probably lose it because you are simply not as strong as your opponent. The trainer must never let it get that far. It is therefore important to foresee and nip all rebelliousness in the bud. You can achieve this through consistency, or in an emergency (if you were not consistent enough or the horse has refused to accept it) by punitive measures. It will be painful to a trainer, if he has to use forceful methods during the adolescent phase of the horse. If he does not want to have to punish the horse constantly later on, however, consistent handling during this phase is essential. This does not

mean, of course, that the horse has to be punished constantly. It can be quite enough to use the voice in admonition or raise your hand, to call the horse to order, but any measure must be applied immediately, as soon as the horse shows any sign of rebellion. The sooner it is nipped in the bud, the less often forceful methods have to be used. If you keep up the necessary consistency and if the youngster is used to ongoing schooling since it was a yearling, it will require few punishments. The horse will have to realise at all times that you expect your demands to be taken seriously.

No schooling works solely through punitive measures and admonishments. Rewarding your horse is much more important and should not to be neglected during the difficult phase of your horse's training. You must take every opportunity to praise the horse. Praise is the means used to keep punitive measures to a minimum, because the horse will always opt more often for behaviour which is rewarded rather than punished. The horse will always take the easier and more pleasant path. Therefore it is a basic principle in training a horse to make it difficult for the horse to react in an undesirable fashion and to make it easy for it to behave correctly.

When schooling and training horses, praise is more important than punishment.

The whip serves as an extension of the arm. The horse should not show any fear of it and allow itself to be touched all over without becoming afraid.

INTENSIFYING OBEDIENCE AND DISCIPLINE

The lessons already learned can suddenly present themselves as a new challenge, if the horse shows no interest in performing its tasks. It can sometimes be very frustrating if the simplest of exercises no longer succeeds, because the young horse is trying to rebel. However, you should use this opportunity to consolidate the young horse's obedience and discipline. The horse is now able to concentrate for a longer period (about 20 to 30 minutes), which means that intensive and consistent work is the best method to put the horse's education onto a firm foundation. The lessons, which the young horse should learn in its third year, will prepare it for backing. Although you may not establish the relationship between many of the exercises and riding yet, they are nevertheless irreplaceable as a foundation.

TRANSFERRING TO VERBAL INSTRUCTIONS

The leading lessons the young horse has learned so far should now be built on, through further training. The two-year-old horse knows the lead-rope with chain from its first independent excursions on the lead-rope outside the yard. It has also probably been made familiar with the whip, which will be indispensable for ground work, because the trainer's arms can no longer embrace the horse, which has grown considerably in two years. The whip represents the extension of the arm and serves primarily as an aid. Only in certain exceptional circumstances should it be applied as an instrument of punishment.

If the horse did not have the opportunity to get to know the whip, it will be familiarised with it now. If the use of the whip as an aid is to succeed, the horse should not exhibit any fear of it. Normally foals which have been desensitised by their previous training will let their trainer touch them all over without becoming afraid. They learned this during the sacking out training, which should also now be intensified (see p. 108 ff.). Well-prepared two-year-olds should have no problem with being touched all over with the whip, and show no defensive reaction. The whip is used to stroke the whole horse beginning with the neck and not forgetting the stomach and the inside of the legs. If the horse stands during this procedure the whip may be used as an aid. If the young horse, however, shows any fear or uncertainty, the whip was probably too often incorrectly applied as an instrument of punishment, or the foal has not built up sufficient trust in the trainer.

Up to now the horse on the lead-rope always started moving, when the person leading it set off. Horses communicate primarily through body language. As they don't know any other means of communication, they rely on body language when humans handle them. That means that the horse focuses on the human's stance and movements, in order to respond to him/her. If the leading human walks on, it follows.

With regard to the preparation as a riding or carriage horse, this is the time to start schooling the horse not to react to body language but to take verbal instructions from its trainer. Due to the limited influence the driver has on them, carriage horses are trained mainly through voice commands. The voice is equally important for the riding horse, because it can be used to help the horse understand the leg and rein aids, which to a certain degree can only be taught from the ground.

> The transfer from using body language to verbal communication makes the schooling of the horse much easier.

If the horse has learned to trot simply by giving it the voice command (for example: "Teeerot"), an obedient horse will follow the

The starting position for leading.

On giving the voice command, the horse should start moving off, before the leading person has actually set off himself. This is the only way to guarantee that the horse is reacting to the voice command alone.

command without any other aids and start to trot. If you later sit in the saddle of an unschooled horse, you can then use the voice just as well as you have done from the ground, meaning that you can control it even though it knows nothing about leg and rein aids.

Combining the leg and rein aids with the familiar voice commands, is the fastest way for the horse to learn what the various aids mean. By linking the two, the horse will not have to learn by bad experience, usually expressed as a punishment, if it responds incorrectly to an unknown leg aid. Using primarily the voice will help strengthen trust and improve the attention of the youngster. After all, if the voice is used as a punishment (loud and harsh words), this does not harm the horse physically. In addition, the sensitivity with regard to leg and rein aids is retained.

As soon as the young animal has learned the verbal instructions for all necessary movements, it is theoretically possible to ride the horse after getting it used to the saddle and bridle. Thus, this lesson is one of the most important chapters in the schooling and training of the foal.

It is the trainer's task to translate the aids from body language to verbal commands. This is also achieved by combining the familiar body language with the voice commands, which are still incomprehensible to the horse. In order to teach it to respond only to verbal instructions, this body language must come first. In practice this works as follows: the leading human stands level with the horse's shoulder and takes the lead-rope about 30 cm from where it attaches to the headcollar. However, the trainer does not simply move off and expect that the horse will follow, as most foal owners have been doing up to now. Instead you give the young animal the voice command to walk on (for example, "Walk on!"), wait for two seconds to elapse and only then move off on your own.

During the first few times you give the command, the horse will almost certainly not immediately march forward, but will wait until you move off. It will, however, combine the command with the desired reaction the more often you repeat it. It will only be a matter of time until the horse will respond simply on hearing the command.

This exercise will not work if you yourself move off too early! The animal needs two seconds to respond and associate the command with the movement. Before supporting the exercise with body language (in this case: moving off yourself), the horse is assisted further after the verbal instruction and the two-second reaction time, with a gentle tug on the lead-rope, a gentle touch with the whip on its hind hand, as well as with the frequent repetition of the spoken command.

Once the exercise succeeds, you must praise the clever horse profusely. From now on you should not lead by starting off first, if you use the voice to ask the horse to walk on. Thereby the voice command becomes the priority aid.

STOPPING

The vocal aid will already have been applied during training to teach the horse to stand still and is often used unconsciously or automatically by many horse owners as an accompanying aid. The reason is that the person uses verbal language as his main method of communication. However, for horse schooling it is not only important that the voice is used, but also how and when it is used. It is only possible to make the meaning of the words clear to the horse, by using the correct intonation and also by choosing the appropriate moment. Thus verbal instruction, followed by a response time, must always be the first aid. If more support is necessary, the rein (lead-rope), whip and finally body language can be applied. However, the aim is to get the horse to respond to the voice commands alone.

The tone of voice used to give the command also plays a role. The horse will disregard commands given in passing, or in a whisper. If the command is given too abruptly and sharply, the animal could take fright and therefore not respond properly. The instruction must be received by the horse as such. A certain tone with clear enunciation is necessary to transfer the command successfully. Only after responding to voice commands has become part of the horse's nature, will a simple whisper be sufficient for the horse to obey.

After moving off has been learned, the next logical step is to teach the young horse to stop. The principle of the exercise is absolutely identical with that of moving forward.

First give the voice command, for example "Stand" or "Whoa". Always choose the same word for a movement, in order not to confuse the horse. Again you must wait for the obligatory two seconds to give the horse the chance to respond to the verbal command. Initially the exercise does not normally succeed, so you will have to repeat the verbal command and give the lead-rope a slight tug at the same time. In addition, you should move the whip in a horizontal position in front of horse's nose in order to prevent it from moving forward. If the horse now halts, you should continue to walk on for two or three steps, with the lead-rope quite loose. You can also turn around to face the horse and stand in front of it to underline the command.

The horse will stop and stand still on hearing the voice command, even though the trainer walks on. As a supporting measure you can stand in front of the horse facing it at the end of the exercise, to prevent it from moving forward.

If the young horse will not stand, you can use body language as a last resort, and come to a halt yourself. If the exercise is repeated a few times, the horse will soon stop on hearing the vocal command. It is important, however, never to lose patience. Some horses simply require more repetitions until they understand. At the same time, once a horse has learned an exercise properly it will not forget it in a hurry. It can be more frustrating, if the horse picks up things quickly, only to have forgotten everything by the next day, so that it appears that the trainer has to start again from scratch. Apart from that the lesson will only succeed if the horse always gives its trainer its undivided attention.

GROUND TYING

If the young horse knows the command to stand still, it needs to obey this instruction until another command is given. Therefore every step the horse takes must be corrected consistently, by taking the horse right back to the place where it was given the command to halt. The youngster learned to stand still as a yearling and you can now expand on this by moving away from the horse, when it is not tied up. This exercise is called ground tying.

For this purpose, you take the horse into the schooling area, give it the command to stop, then praise it, allowing the lead-rope to fall to the ground, and initially move along the youngster towards its hind hand, making sure to maintain hand contact. If the youngster decides at this point to run away, you must pick up the lead-rope, take the animal back to its place and demand that it stands still again. This routine is repeated until the foal realises that running away is futile. If the task of walking around the horse maintaining constant contact succeeds, without the youngster moving away, the exercise can be made more difficult by moving further away from the horse. For this purpose, first take a few steps back standing directly in front of the animal. This creates an obstacle with your own body. Later on you can walk in circles around the horse (around five metres), without the horse walking away. To begin with, you can use a longer rope or lunge rein in order not to have to let the horse go, and at the same time increase your distance to a few metres.

The trainer can now expand the lesson of stopping, by moving further and further away from the horse. Finally the lead-rope can even be released, while the horse obediently stands still.

This is how the correctly schooled horse stands when it has been ground-tied.

Intelligent horses cannot be left standing loose unsupervised even after the training session has become more advanced, as they know precisely when humans can no longer control them. Eye contact spells control! That is why it should never be broken. On the other hand, leaving a horse on its own out of sight goes against the necessary safety requirements for handling horses. Even if the schooling takes place in a fenced off area, a horse moving around freely could still step on the lead-rope and injure itself, if the trainer does not intervene quickly enough. Therefore, you must never lose control over the animal.

MOVING BACKWARDS

Moving backwards is an important lesson, often demanded under the saddle. Many dressage movements demand this exercise and trail riders in particular must own a horse, which can be directed backwards willingly. In addition, we use this exercise to guide the horse from the ground, and last but not least to increase its obedience. In the wild, horses will move backward to display stepping to one side and giving way. It is a sign of subordination towards a higher ranking member of the herd. Therefore this exercise is very suitable for disciplining the animal, something the two-year-old needs frequently. At the same time making the horse back away should never be used as a means of punishment. The line between calling a horse to order and punishing it is very fine. There is a clear distinction, however, between a corrective and a punitive effect.

> Moving backwards is a valuable exercise for disciplining young horses. However, making the horse back away should not to be used as a means of punishment.

A horse, which has to move backwards as a punishment, will never carry out the manoeuvre well or with pleasure. The aim, however, is for the horse to back quickly and in a relaxed manner whereby the back is arched up (bascule) and the horse can transfer its weight onto the hind legs with its hoofs well under the body. If backing is tortuous and forced, on the other hand, the horse will raise its head and avoid using its hind legs properly by pushing down its back. To begin with, the horse needs to realise what we want from it. For this purpose, the trainer stands in front of the horse and slightly to one side, looking towards the tail. Again, the verbal command which will be the most important aid for this movement in the future, is used first. After giving the command, the trainer waits for two seconds, repeats the command, gives the lead-rope a light tug and taps the horse's breast lightly with the whip. Initially it is probably easier to use the hand as an aid, by pressing the fingers against the chest to the side of the shoulder joint muscle. Most horses are sensitive in this area and therefore move away quickly.

If the horse moves back one or two steps, you should stop the exercise and ask it to stand still using the command it already knows. It is a big mistake to make the horse take as many steps backwards as possible, because all this will achieve is that the horse will be increasingly reluctant to move backwards and will thus become hesitant and unwilling. Therefore you should always ask for fewer steps than the horse is offering to take. The number of steps can be increased as training advances.

At a later stage, you will be able to dispense with rein and whip aids, as long as you always ensure that the foal reacts primarily to the verbal command. If the foal does this, don't forget to praise it profusely. In the end, you will be able to get the horse to back several metres on a long lead-rope or lunge rein, whilst you stay in the same position. A further advance-

Sacking out can be expanded with many types of objects. A gymnastic ball is very suitable for this and can eventually be rolled under the stomach. It is possible to play horse soccer later on.

ment of this exercise is not even use a lead-rope to link you with the horse. If the commands such as standing still, moving backwards and walking on have become routine, you will be able to direct the horse from a distance in the (fenced-in!) schooling area: walking forward, stopping, moving backwards, stopping, and so on. This, however, can only be accomplished with a very safe and obedient horse.

SACKING OUT TRAINING

In order to make lessons more interesting, a sacking out lesson can be scheduled now and again. Since the horse has learned to accept being touched by all kinds of rugs, bags and tarpaulins, it can move on to greater things from here. This is the stage, for example, for introducing the famous rattling bag. Use a jute or plastic bag and fill it with empty cans. The foal is allowed to sniff at it, before you gently stroke the bag along its neck. Keep the lead-rope in the hand, as the foal should not to be tied up for safety reasons. Sacking out is carried out in a place which offers a lot of space (not in the loose box!), is secure (not in the yard in front of the stables with pitchforks lying around) and is fenced in. So the best place to choose is the paddock, outdoor arena or indoor school.

If the young horse accepts being touched with the rattling bag without showing any fear, the noise level can be raised, by gently

A horse that tolerates the rustling plastic tarpaulin over its back, has great trust. As a rule these horses will also allow you to saddle them for the very first time without a problem.

shaking the bag. Finally the horse should be able to tolerate having the rattling bag on its back as well as under its stomach.

The same exercises are carried out with other objects such as gymnastic balls.

If the horse stands still, a large rubber ball used for gymnastics with a diameter of about 65cm is rolled under its stomach. Most horses are extremely uneasy when the ball is under-

neath them. Remember that the stomach is a particularly sensitive area, which the horse tries to protect at all costs. If the gymnastic ball were a predator the horse would be in grave danger. Every unknown object is initially categorised as being dangerous – no wonder it feels uneasy.

Once the horse has gained enough confidence, it will also be possible to pull large tarpaulins across its back and even over its head, without making it panic. You must remember, however, that horses can respond differently every day (up and down days) and that a differently coloured tarpaulin will mean a completely different situation to the foal. It may well be that you will have to start the whole process of sacking out from scratch in this case. On the other hand the horse will begin to accept conditions more quickly and with fewer problems with each lesson. The previous training is in no way fruitless.

The sacking out training is also a sensible preparation for backing the horse as it will be more inclined to tolerate the saddle and rider on its back without playing up. Desensitisation also has another advantage. Particularly brash two-year-olds can be brought back under control very quickly with this training. You can guarantee that they will be less rebel-

lious, once they discover that the protection and care of the human being is something they can really use. They learn very quickly that it is much better to trust the owner and follow his/her instructions.

The cockiness of particularly brash two-year-olds can be restrained with sacking out training.

GYMNASTIC EXERCISES

The following lessons are good preliminaries for practising the movements without problems in the saddle later on. The exercises supple up the horse and prepare it for its tasks as a riding horse. Above all it learns to co-ordinate its legs, which results in rhythmic paces and a better balance. Body control is increased and this is an advantage for all later movements. Last but not least, gymnastic exercises also serve to increase obedience and the ability to concentrate.

POLE WORK

Very simple but especially effective exercises are those where the horse has to walk over

Walking over poles helps the horse achieve better rhythm and increases its co-ordination. In addition, the mobility of the joints is improved.

As the horse cannot see where it is stepping, the trainer has a great responsibility whilst asking the horse to back and must guide it carefully.

poles. The lesson should be started with a single pole lying on the ground.

The horse is led over this. In order to avoid injuries to the legs, a fairly high risk in the case of beginners' clumsiness, the horse's legs should be bandaged. Most injuries occur due to knocking the poles, but also through stumbling. Boots provide a good protection.

If the horse is led over a pole lying on the ground, make sure that it registers the obstacle. For this purpose it needs to lower its head.

If the young horse is not paying attention, stop it over the pole and tap the obstacle with the whip, in order to gain the foal's interest. It should not cross the pole until it has dropped its head.

If the exercise succeeds, between two and four poles are laid on the ground parallel to each other and the same exercise is repeated. The distance between the poles must suit the length of the horse's stride, so that the exercise does not become too difficult. Ideally, the horse should keep its head lowered while crossing the poles. The youngster needs to keep its eyes on the poles even if the exercise is repeated several times. It goes without saying that you must remember to praise the horse profusely if it has taken care to perform the exercise well.

The gymnastic benefit of the exercise is that the horse has to lift its legs higher than usual. This means that the joints are bent more acutely and become more supple and the muscles are also strengthened, because they have to work harder. Due to the prescribed length of stride dictated by the distance between the poles, the tempo of the walk becomes more rhythmic. You can work on the rhythmic tempo of the paces even more thoroughly in the trot. The distance between the poles is increased to between 60 and 100 centimetres (according to the length of stride and size of the horse). The horse should be able to tread comfortably into the gaps. Horses with a strong predisposition for the pass (frequent in trotters and four-or-five-pace breeds) can improve their diagonal two-legged support required for a rhythmic trot.

Horses also learn to bascule during pole training, which can be also be done in the canter on the lunge or under the saddle at a later stage. The leg action is improved and the animal becomes generally more agile and mobile. This training is not only suitable for young horses, which are trained on the lead, but also for riding and old horses, in order to maintain and improve their mobility. The effect of pole training can be intensified by slightly raising the poles. Cavalettis, however, should only to be used once the horse has sufficient condition and skill. If the young horse becomes tired, the danger of injury through stumbling is very great. It is best not to use raised poles until the horse is being exercised on the lunge rein, which helps improve its condition.

THE LABYRINTH

The agility of the horse can also be trained by leading it down a narrow lane constructed from jumping poles. The distance between the poles should be about one metre, but this can be increased or decreased according to the level of the horse's training and suppleness. Leading the horse along a straight line does not require any particular ability, therefore turns are included, which range from a slight bend to a sharp-angled corner. If the horse is led round the corner, it has to bend around its own longitudinal axis, to stay in the lane. This has an outstanding gymnastic effect.

Incidentally, leading the horse from the ground should be done from the near- as well as the offside. Otherwise, the horse will become too fixated on one side, so that you end up with a horse schooled only on one side long before you even mount it for the first time. People are not accustomed to leading from the offside either, so you can see how difficult such a task can be, if it has to be done on the untrained side.

The labyrinth can be made more elaborate the more observant and able to concentrate the horse becomes. You can use this not only for leading the horse forward, but also as an ideal training instrument for practising moving backwards between the poles. In order to ensure that the horse does not lose interest in the exercise, any backing between the poles should never last too long. Note that the horse should not touch the poles. The youngster should be able to rely on its trainer, who is leading it through the poles, for it will not be able to see where it is going. Proof that the horse trusts its trainer is if the young horse moves back on command without hesitating. If the two-year-old tends to veer off to one side with its hindquarters, corrective action must be taken. The easiest way to do this is to push the horse's head over to the side to which the horse is veering

At the corner of the L-shaped labyrinth, the horse must carry out a combined turn on the forehand and haunches. For this to succeed the aids have to be finely tuned.

off. The animal always endeavours to keep its body straight and will therefore bring its back legs back onto the proper track. In corners the horse will have to carry out a combination of a turn on the forehand and the haunches, in order to accomplish out this difficult movement. If the animal experiences difficulties, the separate sideways movements of its hindquarters and forehand should initially be practised without poles.

DEVELOPING SIDE-TRACKING MOVEMENTS

It is simpler for a horse to carry out a turn on the forehand, where the hindquarters move around the stationary forehand. The reason for this is that the horse transfers its weight on the forehand rather than the hindquarters. The hindquarters serve as a thrust instrument, the forehand as a support. For this reason the horse, in a natural position, stands with about two-thirds of its weight on its forehand and one third on its hindquarters. It is, therefore, easier for the horse to move the hindquarters around the forehand than vice-versa. Since a rider seeks to teach the horse to place more weight on its hindquarters in order to relieve the forehand overburdened by the extra weight of the rider, it is better to perform more turns on the haunches during training, from the ground as well as from the saddle.

Nevertheless it is better and easier to begin with the turn on the forehand. For this move-

ment, the trainer turns the horse's head slightly to the left, if the horse is to move to the right with its hindquarters. This makes the exercise more successful since the horse tries to stay in a straight line. Now a light pressure is applied with the finger to the horse's flank, which induces it to move away sideways. As soon as the horse responds, the trainer must break the contact to indicate to the horse, that its reaction was correct. After a few repetitions, lifting the hand or a light touch should be all that is needed for the horse to move away. Naturally, the exercise must be performed on both sides. The vocal command must not be forgotten either, of course, and should be applied as the first aid.

The turn on the haunches is carried out in the same way, only in this case by applying the pressure on the shoulder. The horse's head should be turned against the direction of movement, as this helps the horse move away from the shoulder.

Now both exercises can be combined into a full-pass movement, which means that the horse walks sideways with both fore and hind legs. During the movement the horse keeps its head and body straight. Pressure is applied to the thigh to encourage the horse to move both fore and hind legs away without moving forward. The trainer must make sure that the two-year-old crosses over the respective moving legs in front of the leading legs. For this purpose, the horse must learn to place the leading fore and hindleg back a little, to make room for the legs which are crossing over. If you initially position the forehand slightly in the intended direction of the full pass, it will make it easier for the horse to cross in front of the leading leg. To ensure that the animal does not attempt to move forward, which it will be inclined to try, due to the unusual and difficult movement, the full pass should be practised in front of a fence or wall. If the two-year-old horse is already confident at performing the full pass and can co-ordinate the steps, the exercise can be attempted over a pole. Finally, after the

appropriate training, you will be able to ask the horse to move sideways over a combination of poles. These can be laid out in L, W, or U-shape. Always remember, however, that these exercises require a high degree of concentration, co-ordination and dexterity. Don't therefore practise for too long, but instead let the young horse rest at regular intervals. We all have the tendency to continue with an exercise, especially when the lesson has been going very well. If the

Teaching a horse to move sideways in a full pass has a good gymnastic effect. At the same time this movement should not be exaggerated as it requires a high degree of concentration, co-ordination and dexterity.

horse becomes tired, its concentration will wane and errors will occur. You should always end on a high note which brings satisfaction, and stop before reaching the stage of fatigue, and take the horse back to the field.

THE HORSE DEVELOPS THROUGH THE EXERCISES

After their first lessons as a foal and then a yearling, two-year-olds are often sent out to pasture for a year until they are mature enough to be ridden. If you take into consideration the fact that this is precisely the time which is most important for the development of a horse, you will also see that this period of schooling and training should not be lost. Often it is impossible to control two- to three-year-old horses when they come back from the pasture. They have basically slipped back to being wild. There is no reason for not letting the horse have a rest for a few weeks (for example, if the weather is awful), thereby interrupting the actual training, but you should never break off the horse's contact with humans completely. The horse's feet should be checked daily in any case. Therefore, the horse needs to be brought in every day from the field to have its feet picked out, and to check the horse for injuries. This is also an opportunity to groom it, stroke it, or take it for a walk. These activities are sufficient, if you want to cut back on training.

During the training breaks the horse can relax psychologically, which will certainly profit it, if it has been working very hard. However, as a rule, most horses are not challenged sufficiently, since their owners simply do not have enough time for them. Therefore, deliberately planned training breaks are usually not needed at all. However, the intensity of training also depends on the psychological performance of the horse. Some horses have had their fill after only 15 minutes, others could go on for ever with the tasks they have been given. The horse owner must develop a sense for the right time to stop.

It is normally possible and even sensible, to handle the horse every day. The amount of daily work, however, should not go beyond a certain time limit. It is better to work for 20 minutes every day, than for a two-hour period once a week. This 20-minute period should be spread over three-quarters of an hour to eliminate any stress and you can work with the horse in a calm atmosphere. That way work will be fun and the final result will be satisfying.

It is preferable to work for 20 minutes per day than for two hours on the trot.

Sometimes, a good training atmosphere also increases the horse's performance. Some youngsters are so ambitious and keen on their subject that it is difficult to stop early enough.

Leading a youngster from another horse on the lead-rein remains a good training method for young horses. However, it requires a very well-trained riding horse.

Half an hour can pass by very quickly, but you can stop on a high note and look forward to tomorrow.

EXPANDING THE TRAINING OF THE LEAD-REIN HORSE

There are so many different types of activities which can be done with two-year-olds that you don't have to be afraid of boring your youngster. By now, you will most probably have developed a good relationship with your young horse, and many horse owners can hardly wait to finally back the horse for the first time. But there are some things you have to wait for patiently, for it would be wrong to demand too much of the horse. Apart from that your youngster should be well prepared when the great day finally arrives.

Leading a youngster from another horse on the lead-rein remains a very good preparation for the two-year-old horse, and you should not drop it if there is a riding horse available, as well as the youngster. The riding horse needs to be used to being ridden one-handed, so that the other hand can hold the young horse running alongside. Having a well(!)-trained western ridden horse can be of a great advantage here, because the well-schooled western horse has been taught to neck-rein. This means that the horse responds to the pressure of the rein on the neck by moving away, which makes one-handed riding easy. Neck-reining, however, should not be confused with yanking the horse's head, unfortunately seen so often.

Having a good lead horse, which responds well to voice commands, will enable you to perfect the correct handling of the lead-rein youngster. The more experienced and capable the lead horse is, the simpler it will be to train the young horse on the lead-rein. The young horse's confidence will be greater, because it can follow the example of its older companion.

Start getting used to always giving a clear voice command when changing the pace or tempo. The horse knows these vocal instructions from the groundwork training. Since the ridden horse also responds to these commands, the commands, in connection with the correct reaction, will become automatic. Thus, the lead-rein horse learns the commands out on hacks and – although it will not be as careful and attentive as in the school at home – learns to obey the voice.

Now and again you will very probably have to reinforce the order, by gently pulling on the lead-rope with the free hand. The young horse should learn to walk level with the rider's knee, where it can be controlled most efficiently. In some situations, however, it is necessary for the led horse to follow the rider's mount or even walk in front. If

you have to pass through a narrow gap – for example, if other riders and walkers come from the opposite direction on a narrow country lane – the horses need to walk behind each other, in order to prevent a collision.

It is very useful in this situation to have one hand free to control the young horse. If the two-year-old should walk behind the lead horse, a further voice command is useful. When the path becomes narrow, the young horse sees the need to make way. After passing the narrow gap, the young horse is brought forward again. Again, using the voice as well as the lead- rope should be automatic. Never pull hard on the lead-rope, because the logical reaction for the horse will be to pull back. The impulse with the lead-rope should, on the contrary, be carried out with a gentle tug. A little practice will soon make this an easy task to perform.

To ensure that the lead-rein horse remains attentive and sensitive to the instructions of the rider, the horse is encouraged to alternate walking along beside the lead horse – even if the need is not there – with following it. Make sure that the young horse does not practically try to hang onto your own mount's tail, which is what uncertain horses like to do. Later on such horses will continue to cling to the tail of the horse in front. This is very unpleasant for the rider, because the horse is not in sufficient control and soon develops into a full-blown nappy horse.

Therefore, even a lead-rein youngster needs to become independent. You will be achieve this objective by sending the horse on ahead. For this exercise, the horse walks alongside the mount, which you should, however, only do with horses which get on well together, and a lead-rein horse, which is already easy to control. There is normally no great problem in sending the youngster on ahead at the walk and trot. For reasons of safety alone, however, the led horse should always be kept level with the rider's knee during the canter.

Since the lead-rein horse is also learning the command for cantering at this stage (which hasn't been possible from the ground up to this point), the horse is now familiar with all the basic verbal instructions for basic training under the saddle.

The possibility of exercising the young horse at the trot and canter when out hacking, primarily increases its condition. It promotes the development of muscles and firms up the tendons and ligaments through moderate training. Upping the length of time during which the youngster moves on a straight line, mainly outside the school or yard, helps the youngster find its balance and rhythm. Take care not to upset the horse's tempo in the different paces by pulling on the lead-rope. The lead-rope should be long enough to allow the horse to hold its head in its natural position.

CIRCUS LESSONS

Now the horse is at an age when it can be taught a few tricks in play, which increases its mental flexibility and also promotes the relationship between man and horse. There are a large number of exercises which fall in this category and

you can let your imagination run free. However, choosing between those which are sensible and which are not, needs to be done with care, as there is the danger of teaching the horse vices, if you choose the wrong exercises.

Circus lessons and tricks increase the mental flexibility of the horse and promote the relationship between man and horse.

It is a simple matter to teach the horse how to rear up, but in future this trick will be useless for a riding horse. On the contrary, the horse will have learnt to rebel and defend itself, which in the final instance could prove fatal for the rider. If the horse rears, loses its balance and falls over backwards, the odds are stacked against the rider coming away without injury. Scraping with the hooves is another thing not to be encouraged as this soon teaches a horse to beg that way. It can wear away the toe of the hoof or even learn to kick out with its forelegs. Therefore, the exercises chosen should be tasks which increase flexibility as well as having a gymnastic value.

A simple exercise, which falls into this category, is bowing, which means that the horse tuck down its head between its legs on command. This stretches the horse's top-line. This is a very good exercise not only for young horses but also for older riding horses.

To ensure that the horse knows what is expected of it, the trainer makes an exception to the rule and offers the youngster a titbit

Circus lessons can promote mental flexibility. However, only those exercises should be chosen which have a gymnastic value, for example bowing, which this Arab mare performs simply on a voice command.

from between its forelegs, moving the hand back further and further with each lesson. The exercise is of course accompanied by the appropriate voice command. Therefore, it should be possible to teach the horse after a short time to perform the exercise purely on hearing the verbal command. The training method follows the same principle as teaching the horse to walk on, halt and move backwards. After a successful performance, you can continue to offer the titbit a few more times as a reward (now the reward is not offered under the horse's stomach, but instead after the exercise has been performed). Once the horse is well-schooled enough it should be satisfied with praise. The horse should perform the activity out of obedience rather than as a result of bribery.

A good balancing exercise which is also very good for stretching the ligaments in the neck and back, is the so-called "mountain-goat". For this exercise the horse places both forelegs and hind legs as far as possible underneath its body and then has to keep its balance on the smallest area possible. To do this each leg is tapped with the whip. To begin with, the horse has to learn to raise the leg when it is tapped with the whip. Now the trainer helps the horse to place the leg a little further under its body bit by bit, until all its legs are close enough to each other. This exercise requires a lot of patience and should not be exaggerated to begin with.

You also have the option of practising the "mountain goat" with a pedestal. For this, you will need a circus pedestal with a diameter of about 80 to 120 cm. First of all the horse learns to stand on the pedestal with only its forelegs. Initially it will certainly need help, which consists of lifting the horse's foreleg and placing the hoof on the pedestal. Now the horse needs to place its second foreleg on the pedestal and for this purpose, it is encouraged to take a step forward. Most horses understand this very quickly.

This exercise itself provides a good opportunity to stretch the top-line. Once stepping onto the pedestal with the forelegs has become

a routine, the trainer can now start on the hind legs as he did with the forelegs. One leg is lifted up and placed on the pedestal. Now the horse is encouraged to put weight on this hind leg, which will cause it to bring up the other leg. As this position will initially be very difficult for the horse, it will almost certainly try to climb down. But with a lot of patience and a few training sessions, you should finally succeed.

When working with the pedestal, the horse should always wear boots to ensure that it does not injure itself. If the horse is standing on the pedestal with its forelegs you can ask it to perform a turn on the forehand. This is not as easy as doing it with all four feet on ground as the horse is carrying most of its weight on its hindquarters and is supposed to move them as well. The reverse option of doing the turn with the hindquarters raised is not recommended, as this causes the back to cave in and throw the weight onto the forehand. Another example of a gymnastic exercise is the Spanish Walk. Here, the horse stretches out its forelegs forwards alternately during the walk. This leads to better shoulder mobility. Since the forehand is connected to the main skeleton by muscles and sinews alone, a mobile forehand means that the muscles are relaxed. Usually, relaxed or tense muscles in one part of the body will mean relaxation or tension throughout the whole body. A relaxed forehand will, therefore, also mean a relaxed back and hindquarters.

How does the horse learn the Spanish Walk? The two-year-old should have learned by now to

lift its legs when they are touched by the whip. Now the horse is led forwards at the walk and at the same time the leg which is about to be lifted is touched by the whip. Praise the horse if it performs this step expressively. This "raising the leg slightly higher" will, in the course of time, finally become the Spanish Walk. The horse will raise its foreleg up to the horizontal and even further.

Working with the pedestal will stretch the top-line.

The Spanish Walk is an excellent exercise, which can be carried out later under the saddle, as illustrated here by the author and the Frisian stallion "Pollux".

"FIRST BACKING" AT THE AGE OF THREE

THE PERFORMANCE OF THE YOUNG HORSE

There is continuing debate as to the correct age at which the horse can be asked to perform which tasks. On the one hand, eighteen-month-old foals are broken in so that they can run in their first races at the age of two. Others are backed at the age of two, so that they can start competing in shows at the age of three. Is it all right to use the horse at such an early age?

During the growth phase it is always difficult to assess the conformation of a horse. This three-month-old Quarter Horse colt has shot up at the back, leaving it looking out of proportion.

Each situation must always be seen in context before one passes judgement. For one thing, the maturity of the particular horse must be taken into account and this can vary greatly from breed to breed. In addition, you must always take into account what the young horse can be expected to achieve – physically as well as mentally.

The breeder and professional horse trainer will often push the horse to its limits of performance as they want to optimise expenditure and work to achieve results as much as possible. If the horse is having great success at shows, or is producing good offspring as a brood mare or stud stallion, the earlier the money that has been invested will be returned, the better, and the sooner the horse will make a profit. The trainer also wants to turn horses which are for sale into money as soon as possible, to save on feed bills, space, and work. When money is a factor, the moral issues unfortunately are often ignored. This is as true in the equine business as anywhere else. Any true horse lover will always keep this in mind as a warning. Therefore, it is not always the correct way to proceed as professional horse people do. Hobby riders, who make up the majority of riders, can afford to eliminate the risks of wear and tear and early retirement through premature use simply by waiting a bit longer before expecting great performance from their horse. Anyone who cannot wait due to impatience or who expects too high a performance of a horse out of ignorance risks depriving that horse of some years of its life, because health problems will have been predetermined.

The different ages stated as those at which you can do certain lessons with a horse should only be taken as a reference point as the horse's development is not only determined by its breed but can also vary greatly within the breed. For example, although it is true that one rule of thumb states that a horse should not be burdened with the weight of a rider before its third birthday, this is too early for Iceland ponies because this breed matures very late. As a rule, Iceland ponies are not broken in until they are four or five years old.

CONFORMATION ASSESSMENT

Assessing the conformation can be a big help in estimating the performance capability of a horse. An old saying states that you should assess a horse at the age of three days and then again at the age of three years. The reason for this is that horses grow at very different rates in their stages of development and growth. Yearlings are often overbuilt, as the young animals grow at different rates at the front and back. Growing horses are often disproportionate, their head is too big or small in comparison to the rest of the body, their legs are too long, their neck is too short, and the muscles develop irregularly. From the age of about three, horses tend not to grow much more in height. Their overall height will increase by one to three centimetres at the most. This is the general rule, although I have known three-year-olds grow another ten centimetres in the following three years (until they were really fully grown).

Before the horse is backed, you need to assess it anew to judge its suitability for the intended use and expected performance. The outward appearance tells a lot about potential problems which might arise during various movements under saddle, and can give the trainer a lot of helpful hints to which he should pay heed during further training.

The first view of the horse takes in the outline, which will be either square or rectangular. Short-backed, square horses have fewer problems carrying themselves and bearing their weight on their hindquarters, but they sometimes have problems bending lengthwise. The long-backed horse falls more easily onto its forehand, but at the same time does not tend to overreach with its hind legs.

The next thing to look for is the angle of the joints. A long sloping shoulder, pastern and pelvis will ensure greater mobility. The angle of the pastern should be identical to that of the shoulder and pelvis. Flat or sloping angles usually mean smoother paces because the horse can cushion the motion better. However, this also means that the tendons are under greater stress. A steep angle of shoulder and pelvis means the paces will be uncomfortable, which will stress the tendons less but increase the burden on the joints all the more. Therefore, the ideal case is always the golden mean and, if this cannot be achieved, a more sloping angle is preferable from the technical side of riding. Basically, any extreme will always be negative. An overall harmonious

Outward appearance can only be assessed conclusively in a fully grown horse, like this four-year old Quarter Horse stallion.

conformation, on the other hand, should be of great satisfaction to the owner. Differing angles of hindquarters and forehand are also undesirable. Not only does the horse look awkward but it will also have problems with the rhythmic tempo of its paces. Above all, the horse cannot use the full scope of movement of the more sloping pair of legs due to the limited mobility of the other pair of legs.

Close attention must be paid to the alignment of the legs, as this has a great influence on the performance of a horse. Each incorrect position comes with a unilateral high strain on the respective joint. Usually the hooves will also grow unevenly. The side on which the hoof is steeper is under more strain.

The outward appearance contributes decisively to the use for which the horse is suited. The more specialised and high-level the discipline (racing, high-performance show jumping, dressage and others), the higher the demands placed on having a correct conformation. Naturally, if a leisure horse has a favourable appearance this also helps, but some conformation defects can be accepted provided the defects are taken into account during riding and schooling. Since the expectations of the performance of the horse are lower in the case of horses used solely for leisure riding, conformation defects have less significance. However, you have to remember that these types of defect will always have a detrimental effect on the horse's performance. This needs to be taken into account even during the backing phase, and

The position of the hoof should be observed closely. The steeper side of the hoof (here on the left-hand side) takes the greatest strain.

the horse may need a further six months until you start using it under the saddle.

EARLY AND LATE DEVELOPMENT

The age at which a horse can be worked under the saddle continues to be a subject of discussion.

The outward appearance is one deciding factor, in other words, the assessment of physical growth. In addition, the breed can be used as an assessment criterion, although one should not lump all horses of one breed together. There are so-called early and late maturing breeds. Thoroughbreds, for example, belong to the early maturing breeds, whereas Iceland ponies belong to the late maturing breeds. This means that whereas many thoroughbreds are broken in at the age of two, Iceland ponies are left until the age of four or five. Breeders, of course, tend to go for early maturing breeds in order to keep maintenance costs as low as possible. The early maturity of certain horse breeds is, therefore, also the product of breeding. This is particularly obvious in Thoroughbreds. The horses are selected on the basis of their racing performance. The sooner they are able to achieve top performance, the better the horse. Any horse that successfully survives the punishing demands of training and racing is put out to stud after its racing career so that it can pass on its qualities.

This acceleration of development cannot, however, be continued limitlessly. On the contrary, early maturity incorporates a danger of constitutional weakness and signs of degeneration. Without doubt, the goal of each horse breeder is the performance horse. At the same time the question arises whether a horse which is being bred to perform in equine events can reach a "normal" age. The view that putting a horse in training a year early means several years of premature wear and tear and therefore a shorter life span is borne out. The breeder, again, can only profit from this. The sooner the horses are burnt-out, the sooner he can offload his next batch of offspring. The shorter life span of early maturing horses seems to be borne out by that of late maturing breeds. The Iceland pony is a perfect example, having a natural life expectancy twice that of a warm blood.

Using a horse at an early age will cost it several years of its life because the probability of premature wear and tear is high.

Although the general aim is for a horse capable of good performance, breeding goals are not always the same because of the varying living conditions and uses required of today's domestic horse. This is how a great variety of breeds and types have been developed and become established, all showing varying degrees of maturity at any given age.

This variation needs to be taken into account when using the horse. Age is the best reference point, but needs to be modified by an expert assessment of the physical and psychological development of the horse. All of these factors contribute to deciding whether the young horse will backed at the age of two, three, four or five years.

THE SIGNIFICANCE OF THE GROWTH PLATES

The term growth plate, or epiphyseal plate, refers to the ends of long bones. In these areas bone growth continues as long as the horse is in its growing phase. The bone formation can be seen in an X-ray as joints. Once these joints close at an age of two or three (in the case of late-developing horses), bone growth is complete. From this we may assume that the horse can carry a load and therefore be ridden without any damage occurring. The horse's legs, however, need to be X-rayed in order to confirm completed bone growth. The cost involved means that this option is usually only taken by the professional trainer or breeder. The hobby rider will hardly ever make use of it.

SYSTEMATIC MUSCLE BUILDING

When you have made sure that the horse's growth phase is complete and it has reached its full performance capacity, you should not start strenuous training immediately. This also would simply damage the horse. Each training plan needs to be constructed systematically and gradually intensified. The aim is to prepare the young horse for the psychological as well as physical demands to be made of it during the forthcoming training programme. Unnatural demands will be made of the horse by using it for riding or driving and

if it is not expertly prepared for these strenuous demands the animal will inevitably be overtaxed. Riding horses in particular have to become accustomed to having the weight of a rider on their backs. This requires building up the muscles in the back region to avoid straining the bone structure. The horse can only bear any type of load for which nature did not prepare it (and which therefore also overburdens it) if it has the reserves to compensate for those loads. This is why it is so important to keep the horse in good health and expertly trained.

ROUND PEN AND LUNGEING WORK

As a rule, the physical training of the young horse begins when it is first introduced to the lunge rein. Lungeing work improves condition and builds up the horse's muscles. Further aims of lungeing are teaching the horse to find its balance and rhythm and further development of the paces. To this end, the art of lungeing needs to be performed in an expert manner and not simply degraded to chasing the horse round in circles. Teaching the wrong lungeing techniques can do the horse more harm than good.

Often, the aims of lungeing work can be better achieved in a round pen without the use of a lunge-rein. Working with the lunge unfortunately has its weaknesses, as well as its advantages. Some of the disadvantages of

Useful lungeing work is only possible with the correct equipment, which includes a well-fitting cavesson.

lunge-rein. Lungeing with a stable halter can cause distortion of the cervical spine and this exposes the horse to rotational stress, mainly between the second and third cervical vertebrae. Ultimately, the relaxation of the horse and co-ordination and development of the paces will suffer. As a consequence further stress can occur in various leg and vertebral joints.

Hooking the lunge-rein onto the ring of the snaffle bit has similar effects. In addition, the sensitive mouth of the horse is upset considerably, numbed for no good reason, and the bit is pulled sideways out of the horse's mouth. Therefore, the influence is very imprecise and not well received by the horse. Using a lungeing bridle increases the negative effect on the skeleton and muscles of the horse and merely prevents the bit from being pulled through its mouth. A good, well-fitted cavesson, is therefore a must for lungeing work. Never attempt to lunge with the bit and headcollar.

The round pen completely eliminates the dangers of any stress to the joints, as the trainer can carry out his work without the lunge-rein. Apart from that, the circular, enclosed school prevents the hindquarters breaking away from the circular bend. Many young horses try to keep their bodies straight, as this position is easier for them. The horizontal bending of the horse's body, however, helps achieve a practical gymnastic effect which increases balance and flexibility considerably. During "normal lungeing" work it is very difficult to teach the horse the correct bend, as not very many people can cope with the dou-

lungeing can be eliminated by working in a round pen.

The first step towards sensible lungeing work is the use of the correct equipment. The horse always needs to be fitted with a well-fitting cavesson, which lies high enough on the bridge of the nose. The lunge-rein is hooked onto the front ring. This guarantees that the trainer has a precise point of contact on the horse's mid-axis, which supports the correct bending of the horse on the circular line by means of signals transmitted through the

ble-lunge, which – in the same way as the round pen – restricts the horse's ability to move its hindquarters away from the circular line and makes bending easier. Therefore, the round pen is a commendable all-round solution, having hardly any disadvantages but instead almost only advantages compared to lungeing.

Before the horse is capable of bending sideways, it needs to be able to flex its back muscles up, i.e., bend vertically. For this, the horse needs to have learned the position of relaxation which is achieved through the extension of the horse's top-line forward and downward. After some relaxed warming-up, the horse should adopt the position of relaxation naturally. However, this is only possible under special conditions. The horse must feel at ease and be up to the requirements. If the position of relaxation has been achieved, flexing the back muscles up is the next step. This is achieved by encouraging the horse, with the whip, to place its hind legs further under the body. This leads to the horse bearing more of its weight on the hindquarters, flexing its back muscles up and thereby strengthening

If there is no assistant available, lungeing can start with the lead-rope and whip.

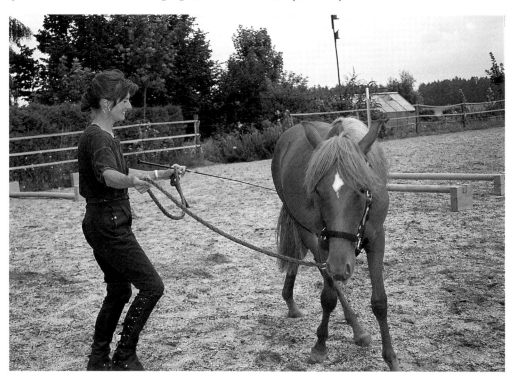

You should move to a circle with a larger diameter as soon as possible to ensure that the horse does not have to bend inward too much.

he/she is doing. Incorrect use of these aids can cause more damage than good. Our young two-and-half-to three-year-old horse should have the look of a fully grown horse before we commence with lungeing. If there is no assistant available, a longer lead-rope and whip should initially be used instead of the lunge-rein. First, request the horse to stand still while you move back two to three metres. Now you can make the young horse walk using the familiar voice command. The whip may also lightly touch the flank if the horse hesitates. In addition, it is permitted to use body language to make it easier for the youngster to understand. One step towards the horse's hindquarters will encourage the animal to move forward. By the same token, forward movement can be stopped by moving towards the horse's shoulder. The neutral position is always level with the horse's middle.

Once the horse has learned to move around its trainer in a circle, the same lesson must be taught on the other rein. As we usually lead the horse from the near side, initial lungeing should also be started on this side. More patience will be necessary on the off side if this side has been neglected during leading lessons.

The size of the lungeing circle can slowly be increased, until you reach a diameter of about 12 metres. If you have an assistant, the larger diameter should be used immediately, and the assistant will lead the horse. The assistant needs to lead the horse to the outside away from the person holding the lunge-rein until the horse realises that it needs to walk in a circle on a slightly tense lunge. The same princi-

these muscles, as well as lengthening its stride (developing the paces). This training prepares the horse to take the weight of the rider and balance the additional load without a problem and, above all, without suffering any damage. Under normal conditions the training of the horse on the lunge-rein or in the round pen can take place without side-reins and other artificial rein aids. Sometimes, however, side-reins can help show the horse the correct way clearly. If you intend to use side or other corrective reins, this should only be done after considerable thought and only over a short period of time. The inexperienced horse-owner should seek help from an expert and by no means try to use additional lungeing equipment or side-reins without knowing what

ple applies to both reins. The commands must be given by the person holding the lunge rein to ensure that the horse concentrates on him from the start.

As soon as the young animal no longer requires a leading person the assistant can hold the lunge whip instead. He moves with the horse in a circle standing a few metres diagonally behind it and using the whip when necessary. In the case of a well-prepared horse, however, additional assistance will hardly be required, because trainer and horse are already a good team.

Always try to move to a large circle as soon as possible so that the horse does not have to bend inward too much. In addition, the horse would have to lean inward on a small circle if the pace is increased, which leads to extreme strain on the joints, ligaments and tendons. In order to prevent excess strain, young horses should be worked on the largest possible circle. At the same time, the lungeing person must not lose control of the horse through the circle being too large.

This marks the only disadvantage of the round pen. The size of the circle cannot not be altered, unlike during lungeing. Due to the preparatory schooling, the trainer has no difficulty in requesting all three basic paces. You have to ensure, however, that the animal carries out each command immediately. For example, it should not "fall" into the canter from an increasingly fast trot, but perform the transition on the spot. For this purpose, the horse needs to use its hindquarters accordingly, and do so even more during a transition from walk to canter. If

it simply changes to a canter from a very fast trot, on the other hand, it will transfer most of its weight onto its forehand, which we want to avoid of course.

> Compared to work on the lunge rein, the round pen has all the advantages, apart from the fact that the diameter of the circle cannot be varied.

PASSIVE BENDING AND STRETCHING EXERCISES

The build-up of muscles as well as mobilisation of the joints can be supported by gymnastic exercises. These exercises should be used, but not abused, in order to train muscles, tendons and ligaments. Such abuse can lead to pulled and strained tendons. The young horse's structure is particularly vulnerable, because it is not trained at this stage. Therefore, training has to be built up slowly and carefully. If the horse has loosened up and warmed-up on the lunge, it can start with light bending and stretching exercises. This is a gentle way to achieve greater agility and has a positive effect on the dexterity, mobility and athletic ability of the horse.

Exercises which also promote athletic ability are introduced in the chapter on practical circus lessons, which, however, consist exclusively of active mobilisation exercises. The passive

Not too much energy should be used to bend the neck to the side. The bend is increased slowly, until the horse's nose touches the stomach.

bending exercises do not require any muscle power on part of the horse, as the trainer moves the respective joint. Thereby, the muscles on the opposite side can be stretched effectively and thus loosened up. This creates the basis for an effective contraction of the respective muscle.

It is important for the rider that his horse can flex its poll. The extent to which the animal can bend its head towards its neck depends on the flexibility of the nuchal ligament and space between the cheeks. To test

the flexibility and improve mobility, the trainer places his hand on the horse's nose and gently presses the head backwards. In so doing the horse flexes between the occipital bone and the first cervical vertebra. Then the neck is bent sideways, an exercise during which the horse can by all means touch the stomach. At the same time no force must be used. If the young horse tenses its muscles the exercise will not succeed. Therefore, a careful handling of the horse is important to retain its trust. Following this, the trainer picks up a front leg, takes hold of the leg above the carpal joint (knee) and brings the forearm up and forward to the horizontal position. The leg should hang freely below the carpal joint. (The horse has no muscles below the carpal joint, only tendons. Therefore, stretching the area below the knee is impractical. In addition, this puts too much of a strain on the front fetlock joint, if you hold the leg by the cannon bone and pull it forward.) This exercise is good for stretching the shoulder muscles, the broad back muscle and the Musculus serratus anterior of the chest. Moving the leg backwards stretches the frontal shoulder area well. Naturally, the exercises must be performed equally on the near- and offside. Then, you should devote time to the hind legs. If you pull a hind leg backwards, the muscles of the iliac bone, the hip as well as the thigh are stretched. These are predominantly muscles which ensure that the horse can bend its leg and bring it forward. If these muscles perform well, the horse will be able to track over better with its hind legs.

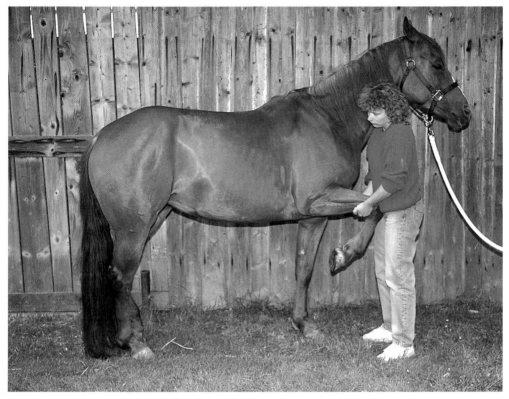

The stomach musculature is stretched when the front leg is raised. To protect the carpal joint (knee), the leg is lifted at the forearm.

In many horses the rear thigh muscles are hypertonic, which means excessively tense. Therefore, relaxing these muscles should be a priority. For this purpose, lift a hind leg, take it above the fetlock joint and bring it forward along the line of its natural movement. Take care that you don't pull the leg outwards, as this could lead to damage to the joints. It is, however, quite possible to pull the leg inwards (underneath the horse's stomach).

These stretching exercises should not be forced to the point where the leg touches the body, as that would be unpleasant for the horse, and it may try to pull the respective leg away.

Stretching is done as far as the horse permits it. Once the horse has learned to trust the exercises, it will not tense up, which means that the stretching exercises can be carried out much more effectively.

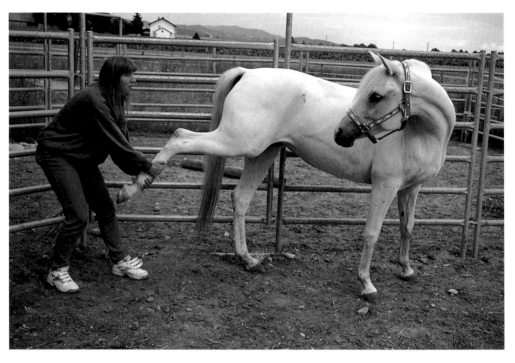

Pulling the hind leg back helps stretch the muscles of the iliac bone, the hip as well as the thigh.

BACKING

The actual breaking-in of a young horse presents no problems, if it is based on a well-founded schooling and consistent training. The training programme presented here prepares horses very well for the initial breaking-in process, so that the initial backing, i.e. the first mounting of the rider, is neither dangerous nor dramatic. I have never had a single horse which I backed myself, which showed any signs of fear or rebelliousness. Instead they could practically be ridden straight away. This has not been the result of any particular strong nerves on the part of the horses (there have been many breeds like cold bloods, Arabs, ponies, trotters, warm bloods, Haflingers, English Thoroughbreds and others more). Instead it has been the result of good preparation. In the case of a foal, you have got three years to do this. Therefore, you should make good use of this time so that the backing and breaking-in process is no longer a difficult subject.

> A thorough preparation of the young horse guarantees backing and breaking-in without a problem.

GETTING USED TO
THE SADDLE AND BRIDLE

Headcollar and cavesson have become routine for the young horse and it is used to having something on its head. Now, however, it is time to create the pre-requisites to transfer precise signals with the reins to the horse's head, which requires a suitable bridle. I personally prefer riding young horses with the bitless Sidepull bridle, because it is hardly distinguishable from the halter and cavesson in terms of comfort, but allows me to convey clear rein aids to the head. For insurance reasons, riding out on hacks with a bitless bridle can sometimes be problematic, so you will soon have to switch to a snaffle bit. As my aim is to start schooling horses out on hacks as soon as possible, I therefore accustom the horse to the snaffle bit before it is backed for the first time.

For its first bitting lesson, the three-year-old wears a normal headcollar with a lead rope attached. The horse is still led and guided with the lead-rope, for initially the snaffle is

only worn so that the horse gets used to having it in its mouth, not in order to transfer any aids on the horse's mouth.

The snaffle mouthpiece lies in the palm of the left hand, by which it is guided to the horse's lips. The right arm and hand cradles the horse's head and holds the cheek pieces. Now, the left hand thumb is pushed into the corner of the mouth and applies light pressure to the horse's bars, which encourages it to open

The Sidepull is an excellent "first" bridle for breaking-in the three-year-old horse.

For a well-prepared horse, placing the saddle on its back presents no problems.

its mouth. The bit is now gently pushed into the mouth, the head piece is pulled over the ears, and finally the throat strap is fastened. Take care that the bit does not hit against the teeth, as this is particularly unpleasant for the young animal, and it can provoke head rearing and other defence reactions.

The bit should just wrinkle the corner of the mouth. If this is the case, the bit is properly fitted. It should not hang too loose in the mouth, as horses tend to put their tongues over the bit or become used to chewing the mouthpiece excessively and pushing it about in the mouth. On the other hand, the bit should not be too tight, as this can cause pain in the corner of the mouth.

The young horse must now try to cope with the bit in its mouth, and it should be left in peace for a few minutes, tied up with the lead-rope. Eventually the bit is removed again. The

next bitting lesson follows the next day. The horse can be taken for a walk or do familiar exercises on the lead-rope while getting used to wearing the bit, but you should not exert any pressure on the snaffle but instead work with the lead-rope.

As the sacking out training was carried out with so many different objects, you can now use the saddle for a change. If the desensitisation process was done expertly, the horse will normally accept having the saddle placed on its back without any resistance. However, fastening the girth is a new experience and must be approached with care, so the horse does not panic or become claustrophobic.

You can also accustom the horse to the pressure of the girth with the aid of a breaking surcingle. Initially, the surcingle is only fastened tight enough to ensure that it will not slip. After a few minutes of letting the horse become used to it, tighten it by one hole. This is as far as you should go on the first day before loosening the surcingle again. In the next lesson, the surcingle can be tightened a further hole. Now you should lead the horse around, so it becomes used to the pressure the surcingle applies while the horse moves. Thus, the horse is slowly accustomed to wearing the surcingle fully fastened and then ultimately the saddle with its girth. Only when the horse accepts the pressure of the girth without resisting it, can the saddled horse be worked as usual on the lunge or lead-rope. Make sure before doing any work that the girth is pulled up tight enough to prevent any slipping.

LONG-REINING AND RID-ING FROM THE GROUND

The bridled and saddled horse is now ready to learn the aids of the rider from the ground. In its previous lessons, the young horse has practised walking on, stopping and changing paces often enough. The primary aim now, however, is to teach the young horse to react to the rein aids. For this the rein is fastened to the Sidepull bridle or cavesson (later to the snaffle ring). Now stand at shoulder level beside the horse and take the reins up the hands, as you would if you were in the saddle. For this purpose, the right hand must be placed on the right side of the withers.

Gentle rein aids in the form of a half-halt are now given on one side. If the horse turns its head to this side, slacken the rein and praise the youngster. This way the horse learns to follow the rein aids. Practise this exercise on both sides. Remember that only by releasing the rein immediately, will the horse respond with increasing sensitivity and soon respond simply to the closing of the fist on the reins.

Now it is time to give the horse the command to walk on. You need to walk beside the horse at shoulder level, which the three-year-old will have to get used to, as the trainer usually stands level with the neck when leading the horse. Normally, the young horses will understand the trainer's intentions quite quickly.

By applying a rein aid while the horse is walking, you can direct the horse in a new direction If a signal is given with the rein whilst walking, then the young animal can be pointed in a new direction: the horse can be guided left or right. Initially, the rein aids are given unilaterally to guide the horse. The horse is ridden from the ground, so to speak, and in this position you can perform all movements learned so far, such as walking, trotting and moving backwards. At the same time, the reins determine the direction of the horse and position of its head.

It is difficult to reach over the withers of a big warm blood. In this case, and with horses which are trained as carriage horses, you can

"Riding from the ground" promotes the horse's independence and teaches it to respond to the rein aids.

Sensitive unilateral rein aids help turn the horse into a corner.

instead long-rein the horse – drive it from the ground. For this purpose long-reins or driving-reins are attached to the bridle and the trainer walks behind the horse. As the animal cannot see the trainer directly behind it, it could possibly become uncertain and try to turn around. In that case it is recommended to walk slightly to one side, so that the horse can keep the trainer in sight. For your own security, long-reining is not recommended for horses which tend to kick. In that case it would be better to do lungeing work on a double-lunge as well as the obligatory, consistent schooling and basic training.

MOUNTING FOR THE FIRST TIME

The young horse has now learned everything, which it needs to master under the saddle, to ensure that the rider and horse will understand each other. The three-year-old horse is now familiar with everything except the rider on its back, which also means an unfamiliar extra weight to worry about. The initial mounting is therefore done slowly and with care, to allow the horse to become accustomed to the weight.

The round pen is an excellent place to mount the horse for the first time. Secure fencing is a must and apart from that the closed-in walls of the round pen will ensure the horse concentrates on the task at hand. The horse will not be able to rush into a corner putting the rider at risk.

To start off, the horse is worked on the lunge or freely in the round pen, to ensure that it is loosened up and relaxed. Then the trainer brings the three-year-old in, takes off the lunge-rein, and places it somewhere safely away from the horse's legs. Slowly put an increasing load in the left stirrup with a hand and observe the horse's reaction. If it remains quiet, place the left foot into the stirrup and slowly transfer weight to it. At this stage it is very helpful if you have an assistant, who can hold the horse by the headcollar and speak calmly to it.

Slowly increase the weight until you can lift the right leg from the ground. In this situation it is particularly important that the girth is fastened properly, so that the saddle won't begin to slide sideways due to the uneven weight distribution. Again, an assistant is an advantage here, as he/she can pull on the right-hand stirrup to provide a certain balance.

If the horse continues to remain calm, you can start putting weight onto the saddle, without at first swinging the right leg over. The day's lesson should end with the trainer sliding back down slowly and putting the horse back out into its field, after praising it extensively. The next day, once you have repeated these exercises, you can proceed to slowly swing the right leg over the horse's back, gently sitting down in the saddle. Do not attempt this step if the horse seems unsettled, but only if it remains completely calm throughout. More lavish praise is now in order. (When swinging the right leg over, make sure you avoid touching the croup with the foot, as this will frighten many horses.) For its first steps under the saddle, the horse is now either led by an assistant or – if you do not have an assistant– encouraged to walk on with the appropriate verbal command. Caution! At this stage any leg aids, i.e., pressure with the calf is inappropriate, as the animal does not understand this aid and could take fright.

Understanding between rider and horse will not be a big problem: after all, the horse has already learned the necessary aids and commands. The greater difficulty for the horse will be trying to keep its balance, and it will therefore move forwards uncertainly and hesitantly. The best way to help the young horse find its balance is to sit in the centre of balance at all times. Weight and leg aids are not applied at

For the first attempt at mounting, more and more weight is transferred carefully to the left stirrup, and at the same time the horse's response is observed constantly.

this stage, because the trainer is in a very good position to guide the horse with voice and rein aids. The horse will learn the other supporting aids via the reins, weight and legs later, once it has found its balance and can carry the rider properly. In the coming time, the horse will be ridden around the riding school in large circles or in straight lines, best done out on hacks.

THE MEASURE OF TRAINING SUCCESS

Sharp corners should be avoided, as they overtax the physical capability of the horse and the balance often suffers too.

The raising, schooling and training of young horses are special experiences, marked by peaks and troughs. No one will want to miss this time, as it is rich in experiences, which primarily cement the friendship and relationship with the horse. Every sensible rider wants his horse to be a friend and comrade, but friendship and trust have to be earned by fair treatment and expert handling. However, the fruits of this work, which is not always simple, are in the final instance enjoyed not only on the show ground or out hacking, but through every handling of the horse, every time it displays its trust and friendship. For this purpose, the horse does not have to be worked under the saddle, as there are a multitude of lessons which a horse should learn before it is backed. This period also teaches the horse lover that riding is not the only practical pastime that can be done with the horse, but that there are a lot of other things, which you can do together with your horse.

The logical structure of the schooling and training plan guarantees that the relationship between man and horse is strengthened through the lessons and tasks performed. Slow patient progress results in greater and certainly longer-lasting success. Therefore it is worthwhile to approach the training of horses with patience and understanding. If a three-year-old horse is unable, psychologically or physically, to carry a rider on its back at this stage, then one should have the courage to postpone this step. It is not a sign of inability if a three-year-old horse is still not ready to wear a saddle instead it shows the trainer's good horse sense in recognising that more time is needed to prepare the horse. It is not the quick education that makes a good trainer, but feeling and consistency!

Buurman-Paul, Ulrike/Paul, Winfried

Moderne Pferdezucht und Haltung

München 1991

Engelmann, Uta/Buurman-Paul, Ulrike

So zieht man Fohlen auf

München 1994

Ettl, Renate

Das Einmaleins der Hufpflege

Stuttgart 1997

Ettl, Renate

**Pferde naturgemäß
und artgerecht halten**

München 1998

Ettl, Renate

**Western Basics –
Die Grundausbildung**

Rüschlikon 1998

Gohl, Christiane

Ein Fohlen aus unserer Stute

Stuttgart 1993

Hoffmann, Marlit

Was tun mit jungen Pferden

Rüschlikon 1978

Kappmeier, Susanne

Ich möchte ein Fohlen haben

München 1998

Lose, M. Phyllis/Meinecke-Tillmann, Sabine

Die Stute und ihr Fohlen

Hamburg 1981

Schäfer, Michael

Die Sprache des Pferdes

Stuttgart 1993

Smythe, Heather

Vom Fohlen zum Reitpferd

Rüschlikon 1999

UNIVERSITY OF LINCOLN